Morphine and De...

Morphine and Dolly Mixtures

Carol-Ann Courtney

Published by Honno

'Ailsa Craig'   Heol y Cawl   Dinas Powys

South Glamorgan   CF6 4AH

First impression 1989

© *Carol-Ann Courtney, 1989*

British Library Cataloguing in Publication Data

Courtney, Carol-Ann

Morphine and dolly mixtures

I. London. Social life, 1950-1969 – Biographies

I. Title

942.1085'5'0924

ISBN 1-870206-09-6

ISBN 1-870206-05-3 pbk

Cover illustration by Tessa Waite

Designed by Ruth Dineen

Typeset in Palatino by Megaron, Cardiff

Printed at the Bath Press, Avon

*In memory of my beloved mother and my father,
whose love I once knew.*

AUTHOR'S NOTE

All characters and events that are depicted in this book are real.
Certain names however have been changed.

ACKNOWLEDGEMENTS

For David, Katie, Simon, Kirstie-Ann, Sam and Ben, also my grandchildren, Charlotte, Daniel and Rachael with the greatest love.

My love and thanks to my many friends past and present who made so many things possible.

Especial thanks to my publishers *Honno* and Rosanne Reeves who has been unwavering in her support at the most painful times during the production of the book.

Last night I met my mother . . . I wave to her as once again she makes her way from under the railway bridge and weaves leisurely up the grassy bank to where I stand, my arms outstretched. I hold her tightly, in an embrace which I am reluctant to break away from; the smell of 'Evening in Paris' combined with Lifebuoy toilet soap pervades my nostrils. I touch her face, her hair.

'Why?' I ask, 'Why did you leave us? — the boys, Anna, my own children' — I name them all — 'my husband. Come with me. Come home, everyone will be so happy.'

'You always ask the same questions, darling, and I can only say it was all too much. This —' she gestures towards the bridge, 'this is where I've been, it's where I belong.'

'No! you belong with us.'

She hugs me briefly. I am angry with her, but she smiles, kissing my mouth before turning to run back down the grassy slope, arms akimbo as if a bird in flight. She waves once more as she disappears through the arch of the bridge. I run down the bank — not as swiftly as she can, but this time I am going to fetch her back. She has played this foolish game far too long. I reach the bridge, looking on both sides at its granite walls. The sun is dancing on the track, which runs on seemingly forever.

'Mummy! Mu-mmy, Mm . . .' The bridge echoes back, mockingly. She has gone, she is hiding down there somewhere, but my eyes have no colour to see. I awake as always — empty, perspiring — but somewhere, at some time, I too have been under that bridge.

1

1

Jean Simmons racing through fog-laden, Victorian London streets, beautiful in her grey cloak, bottom lip trembling — my attention was diverted from the screen by the rasp of a match and the glow as it ignited, only to be quelled again.

'Give it to me, Mummy,' I said in a whisper. 'Ssshh . . .' came from behind us. I put the cigarette in my own mouth and lit it, handing it to my mother, then turned around to the offended party.

'This is disgraceful,' said the patron in the row behind, in a Joyce Grenfell voice.

'Sorry, did you want me to light yours?' I asked. She'd been at the old Butterkist all night, like a regular Bugs Bunny in my ear.

'Don't be rude, darling,' my mother admonished, just as 'Joyce Grenfell' left her seat, with a loud thud, and moved across the aisle to another place.

We'd been waiting a long time to see *Footsteps in the Fog*, with Jean Simmons and Stewart Granger. The yellow footsteps that had been strategically placed around the foyer of the Odeon Picture House had both chilled and excited me, and it had been a treat for me to go with Mummy to see the film. My mother was groping around for an ashtray, and I took the cigarette end from her fingers and extinguished it in the cup-shaped metal tray in front of her.

'Let's go, darling,' she said.

'Go? There's another half hour yet, Mum.'

My mother got up from her seat and I had no choice but to follow. She was holding on to the back of each seat as she made her way up the sloping aisle. Then the brightness of the late spring evening assaulted my eyes and she grasped my hand, leaning a bit heavily.

'It's not bloody fair,' I said. We usually waited until the credits rolled, and made it out before 'God Save the Queen'.

'Don't swear, baby,' she said. 'I'm sorry, I'll make it up to you.'

'You wouldn't have walked out half way through that rubbish you take the boys to,' I grumbled. She was leaning on me so heavily now that we had to stop in the Co-op doorway.

'Light me a cigarette, baby, please.' I took a Player's Weight from the packet and lit it as before, and placed it in her hand.

I was beginning to feel a tremor of fear. In the last eighteen months my baby sister Anna had been born; my mother had undergone brain surgery for a tumour; and I had become familiar with the world of epilepsy. But still it wasn't like Mummy to be so vague and helpless. I remembered my hysteria the first time I saw her in a fit and thought she was dying, as she writhed, her pupils rolled back in her head, revealing white eye sockets. Foam poured from her mouth which was drawn back in a seemingly wicked leer, and as the spasms racked her body, the baby (who had been at her breast) began to fall from her lap. I just managed to save Anna from falling to the floor before I ran out into the street, the new baby under my arm. 'Help me, my mummy's dying,' I screamed.

By now phenobarbitone and morphine had been abbreviated to 'phenos' and 'morphs'. I knew the procedure to use during my mother's fits — loosen clothing, try to compress the tongue with a table-spoon (which is easier said than done), and wait for the attack to subside.

Meanwhile my father, who had had a lung removed prior to my mother's surgery and Anna's birth, and had been discharged from the Royal Navy as physically unfit, had also changed. Although he had lost considerable weight, he was still very tall, very dark and handsome, with those vivid light-blue eyes that look so attractive on very dark-haired men; but the romantic figure who had travelled the world and brought us rare and beautiful presents, as well as giving us sheer happiness and pride in his dark uniform, had gone. The days had gone too when he would hold my mother's hand and take us for boat trips along the Thames, or even take us over a ship in dry dock.

Now, if he wasn't drinking, he would send us all scattering to polish floors, clean drains with Lysol, wash windows with a chamois-leather until they gleamed. He would constantly deride my mother's illness as trivial compared to his own, yet if the priest or doctor called while he was in the middle of a 'brainstorm', within seconds he would become the loving, concerned father and husband, calling on God to help him through. The only evidence of his recent behaviour would be a pulse beating wildly in his temple and a tremor in his hands, and he would even use these symptoms to illustrate his own physical and mental pain and his anxiety for us all.

I once remarked to my brother James that our father had not only kissed the Blarney Stone – he'd bloody well swallowed it! He'd overheard me and had used a leather belt (without the buckle, thank God) on my bottom, which felt as if it was on fire for days afterwards.

Now, my mother and I stood in the Co-op doorway, my fear became more acute. She was trying to grind out her cigarette end, which was about two feet away, on the floor.

'Come on, Mum, let's go', I said. We were half-way across the main road when she suddenly pulled me forward with her into the path of an oncoming bus.

'Mummy!' I screamed. The bus screeched to a halt – the passengers must have been thrown forward in their seats.

'You stupid cow!' the driver yelled. 'If yer wanna git yerself killed, yer goin' the right way about it, lady!'

'I'm sorry.' She seemed to be speaking to no one and everyone.

'We're nearly home, Mum,' I said, as we walked up the hallway to our flat. Gran would be there, thank God. We'd left the boys, James, Patrick and Tim, with her – as well as the baby.

As we made our way along the passage, my mother asked to go to the toilet. She was still leaning heavily on me. Somehow, between us, we managed to get her pants down, and she sat, slightly askew, on the toilet seat.

'Put the light on, darling,' she said.

'Mummy, the light *is* on,' I said, my fear accelerating. I'd called for Gran as we came in through the door, but she'd probably dozed off; now I called again. 'Gran, Granny, come quickly.' There was still no answer.

'Oh my God, baby, I can't see, I can't see!' Panic was rising in her voice.

'Oh please help me,' I screamed, as I walked up the narrow passage way to the toilet. 'I'll have to get help, Mummy, can you sit there?'

'Yes darling.'

'Whas the friggin' fuss for now?' My father's voice from the toilet door made us both jump.

'Mummy can't see.' I shrilled.

'So it's not yer head now, Irene, it's yer bloody eyes, is it?'

'Terence, please help me – where's Gran, I want Gran.'

'I sent yer mother home'.

'Terence, please help me.' She was crying now.

'Well, yer've had a little growth taken outa yer head, an' yer got a little migraine, have yer, darlin'? Well, I've had a friggin' lung taken out, an' yer don't hear me complainin' an' whinin.'

'Oh my babies,' she sobbed.

'Well, yer got one of yer babies fussin' over yer enough now!' He swayed forward slightly and turned out of the door, walking away down the passage.

Somehow we dragged our way up, through the toilet doorway and out through the passage to the front room opposite, where we managed to get her on to the brown velvet put-u-up. I lay across her feet, trying to control my breath – the final effort of swinging her feet over on to the bed-settee had sapped my strength.

'Can you see yet, Mummy?' I asked.

'No darling.'

I ran into her bedroom and took the eiderdown and her pillow off her bed. Baby Anna was still fast asleep in her cot. I lifted my mother's head, and placed her pillow under it, then took off her white sandals and put the eiderdown over her.

'Is the baby OK?' she asked.

'Yes, sound asleep.'

'Are the boys all right?'

'I'll go and get you a cup of tea, Mum, and have a look at them.' I peeped into the boys' room.

'Caroline,' whispered James, 'what's going on?'

'Mummy's not well,' I said.

'Is it a fit?' asked James.

'Sort of.'

'He's drunk,' James said.

'Yes, I know, Jimmy. Try to go to sleep.'

I went into the kitchen. Father sat at the kitchen table, drinking tea and eating a sandwich. 'Has the sight returned?' he scoffed.

'No.' I poured a cup of tea for her, and reached up for her tablets on the top of the kitchen cabinet, then filled a cup with water and took the tablets and the water into the front room. She was still crying, but softly now. I went back for her cup of tea and slipped ten Players up my cardigan sleeve.

'Two phenos, Mummy?' I asked. She nodded. I put the tablets into her mouth and held the cup of water to her lips; she grimaced and swallowed. 'Two morphs?' I asked.

'Yes darling.' I placed the first tablet on her tongue and put the cup to her lips. She swallowed it back, but when I placed the other tablet on her tongue, she spat it out.

'It's saccharin,' she said. I emptied some of the tablets into my palm, and touched three with my tongue. They were sickly sweet, but the fourth was bitter, and when I put it on her tongue, she swallowed it down with the remainder of the water. Then I brought the cup of tea up to her lips, and she drank it straight down.

'Can you see yet, Mummy?' I asked, for the hundredth time.

'No, baby. Did I have a fit?'

'No.'

'Well, it may just be the epilepsy, and my sight will come back.'

My father had just made himself more tea as I took her cup through to the scullery. 'Well, Florence Nightingale,' he said, 'I never saw yer in such a lather about me – an' just look, will yer – here, take a friggin' look.'

He lifted up his shirt at the back to expose a livid scar which ran from his shoulder blade in a curve towards his side. I'd seen it often enough, since he walked around with his shirt off whenever possible, and it always reminded me of a big fish bone.

'Yes, I know, it's horrible, terrible!' I said, placatingly. When I got back into the front room, my mother's sobbing was terrifying.

'Oh darling,' she whispered, 'my legs – I want to go to the toilet, but I can't move my legs.'

I ran into the kitchen. 'Please come,' I cried.

'No. I'm sure yer doin' a great job. Yer Mammy's a great play-actor, yer know.'

I ran into the toilet then, and brought out Anna's potty. I tried to lift my mother on to it as well as I could, holding the wide opening of her pants apart; some urine trickled into the potty, but most of it had spilled on to the settee. As I straightened up, my spine felt paralysed, then the paralysis was followed by a painful, throbbing start.

'I've wet, darling,' she said. 'I've wet the settee.'

'No, Mummy, it's only a bit.' I brought one of Anna's nappies through, and between us we tucked it under her bottom. Then I opened the front door and ran, hell for leather, down along the high street and up the tree-lined avenue where Dr Scanlon lived. I kept my finger on his bell.

'All right, all right, have a bit of patience.' It seemed to take ages for the different locks to be released.

'Mrs Scanlon!' I panted. 'Is the doctor here?'

'What is it, Brigette?' The doctor was on the stairs.

'It's the O'Farrell girl, Gerry.'

'Please, please help me,' I gasped. It's my mummy, doctor, she can't see any more, and she can't feel her legs. Please come!'

'We'll be there in two shakes,' he said, putting on his coat.

'You do believe me, don't you?' I pleaded.

'I wouldn't be hurrying like this if I didn't, child.'

'*He* doesn't believe us,' I sobbed.

'Your daddy, do you mean?'

'Yes, it's been awful.'

The doctor walked briskly, and I was half running, trying to keep up with him.

'Well now,' he said, 'have you not thought that perhaps your Daddy is being a bit of an old ostrich and burying his head in the sand? What I mean is, he doesn't want to believe it.'

At home the front door was closed, and Dr Scanlon knocked sharply. There was no answer, and he rapped urgently again. Inside, a door creaked open, and footsteps came up the hall; my father was half asleep.

'Well, doctor, come in,' he said, pumping the doctor's hand.

'Hello, Terry,' the doctor said. 'It's young Irene, then?'

'Yes. But she's sleeping now.'

'Well, let's take a look at her, shall we?'

'Go put the kettle on, darlin',' my father said to me. 'I'm sure the doctor would like a cup of tea. Did we get you out of bed, Doc?'

'No,' answered the doctor. 'I've been having a lazy evening. — And no tea for me, though I suggest you make yourself a hot drink, m'dear,' he said to me.

They went into the front room and closed the door, and I went into the kitchen and made a pot of tea, then sat at the kitchen table as my father had done earlier. After about half an hour he and the doctor came into the kitchen;

my father was looking an awful colour, and reaching in the cupboard, he brought out a half bottle of rum.

'Go to bed now, darlin',' he said, kissing me.

'You're a good wee thing, Caroline,' said the doctor, patting me on the head. 'God bless now.'

I left the room, and crept into the front room to see if Mummy was awake. She was, and I asked, 'Mum, can you see yet?'

'No, darling, not yet.'

'Are your legs better?'

'No, but the doctor says maybe this will pass in a couple of days. Thank you for going to get him – though I wouldn't have let you, you know.'

'No, I know.' I said. 'But I'm glad I did. Do you want a cup of tea or a cigarette?'

'No thank you, baby. I've had an injection, so I feel all nice and warm and floaty. You go to bed – don't get up for school in the morning. You never know, your old mum might just walk in with a cup of tea for you herself – and, darling, thank you for everything. We'll go and see *Footsteps in the Fog* again when I'm better.'

But there were to be no more footsteps. She would remain in that fog for the rest of her life.

2

It was about ten o'clock the next morning when I was awoken by men's voices outside the bedroom door. I remembered then what had happened the previous night; the other two beds had been made, and as I saw this, I scrambled quickly out of my own bed and into my school uniform, and then made for the door. The doctor and my father were in conversation, and it occurred to me that perhaps the doctor hadn't gone home all night.

'Did you sleep well, darlin'?' my father asked.

'She looks a lot better than she did last night,' said Dr Scanlon, touching my hair.

'The boys are in school and Granny took Anna to the nursery. Your Mammy's having a wash.'

'In the scullery?' I asked, hopefully.

'No.' The doctor was short with me. 'Now, be off into the kitchen with you, and get your grandma to make you some breakfast,' he said, less harshly. 'I just want a few more words with your Daddy.'

I walked down the hall into the kitchen.

'Hello, my princess,' Gran said. 'I hear you were Granny's brave girl last night.'

'Where's Mummy?' I asked.

'That Nurse Parker is giving her a wash down.'

I remembered Nurse Parker from before. She was nice, and had brought me some jumpers and shoes her daughter had outgrown. Gran pottered out into the scullery, and came back bringing with her our enormous enamel teapot and a bottle of cows' milk which she emptied into our one and only jug (a cracked one even so). Next she carried in the glass sugar bowl, full of sugar-cubes, and the sugar-tongs; then, setting two cracked cups and saucers aside for us, she set out another three uncracked cups and saucers and brought in a bowl of cornflakes for me.

'Acting like Burlington Bertie this morning!' she said, as my eyes widened at the plate of Nice biscuits which was set down next.

'Gran, can Mummy see yet?' I asked.

Gran took a green packet of Woodbines out of her pocket and lit one. 'Well, not yet, princess – but I know my girl, she'll get better. You wait and see. And it won't be any thanks to that damned Mick! I *told* her – oh, how many times did I tell her? 'You can do a lot better than that, Irene', I said, 'You're only sixteen, he won't bring you a day's happiness.' But she wouldn't listen to Granny – headstrong, that's what she is, always was, and always will be where *he's* concerned. Drunk, was he?' Her voice lowered. (Gran had always thought the rest of the world was deaf.)

'Yes, Gran. Can she walk yet?'

'No, but the specialist is coming from Hammersmith to see her today.

– Gives me a shopping list as long as your arm, *he* does.' She gestured towards the table, which yesterday would have held a bottle of sterilized milk and the white tub of saccharins. 'Look,' she said, opening the kitchen cabinet. Eggs were lined in the usually empty rack, like soldiers. There were three packs wrapped in greaseproof paper, and there was butter in the cut-glass butter dish. (I could see the grooves through the glass.) There were tins of soup, peas, butter beans, even a tin of Nescafé; it looked like Christmas.

'Where did it all come from, Gran?'

'Lord Bountiful says to me, "Mother, would you get these things for me on the way back from taking the baby?" ' she explained. 'I read down the list and he said it was all right – "Get it out of the Family Allowance", he says, so that's what I did. – Come on, eat those cornflakes for Gran.'

She put the cups and the plate of biscuits on a silver tray with a linen cloth, and took them through the kitchen door.

'Ask when I can see Mummy, Gran?' I called after her. I put the cornflakes back in the box, nibbled one of the biscuits and drank the tea.

When I took the bowl and cups through to the scullery, I saw that all the silver cutlery and serviette rings had been laid out on the wooden draining board, with a tin of Silvo polish beside them. Our home held a mixture of bygone affluence and contemporary poverty. I liked cleaning the silver, and I thought I would ask Gran if I could polish them when she came back again.

Gran came in, followed by Nurse Parker, who had red, frizzled hair underneath her dark cap, and emerald green eyes. Her pretty face had so many freckles that most of them had joined up!

'Hello, Caroline,' she said – she'd even remembered my name.

'Hello, Nurse,' I replied.

'I hear you've been trying to do me out of my job.'

'When can I see Mummy?' I asked.

'Only a few more minutes, and I'll be done,' she said, pouring bluey-grey water down the sink from the all-purpose white and blue-rimmed enamel bowl, the bottom of which sported four rusting washers.

Gran was looking peeved. 'He wants a word with me.' she said, putting the tray on the kitchen table and bustling out into the hallway. I could hear Gran repeating things to my father in a flat voice. 'Well, Terence,' came her voice, distinct now, 'I don't know if there's enough left on it for all that, but I'll see what I can do.'

The nurse gave me a little hug as she went back out to the front room, then my father put his head around the door. 'Yer Mammy's askin' for yer, darlin',' he said, 'and I've got to have a shave after I've seen Nurse out.' He rubbed his blue chin with his long fingers.

For some reason, I knocked on the front room door. 'Come on in,' the nurse's voice called. She was putting on her blue mac. 'There now, Irene, here she is.'

'Hello baby.' My mother's arms were outstretched, but she seemed to be looking above me.

'Oh, Mummy, are you feeling better now?' I asked. 'I've been waiting so long to see you.'

'I think this lady's had a long wait too,' Nurse Parker said, smiling. 'I'll see you this evening, Irene love – and you too, Caroline. And there's baby Anna too. I expect she's grown.'

'Yes, she walks now,' I said proudly.

I looked through the net curtains onto the street. The day was glorious. Inside, the bed-settee had been folded out into a bed, and a white cot sheet covering the bolster and the pillow case under my mother's head seemed grey by comparison with the light.

'Sit down, darling,' said Mum. 'Listen, Daddy's very sorry for last night, and he loves you very much. Granny knows what happened, but I don't think we should tell anyone else, so shall we forget it? I'm sure Daddy will try to make it up to you. And do you know what? When I'm better, we're going to go on holiday, all of us, to Brighton. Granny took Auntie Ruth and me there lots of times when we were little, and it's lovely.'

'Better than Southend?'

'Yes, much, much better.'

I looked at her face. I could see now that her eyes were different, sort of fixed and yet moving about a bit. They were dark brown. Her nose was straight, and her mouth pretty and full, with corners on her upper lip which tilted up into a natural smile even when she was cross. Her hair had been combed, but already her blue-black curls were denying that smoothing pressure and springing back into their natural place.

Her head had been shaved when she'd first come home from hospital, and the right side of her head sloped downwards, so that you could see her brain pulsating, just as Anna's 'soft spot' on her little head did. She'd had a gauze covering on then and still always wore a headscarf whenever she went out, even now. She called the sloping side of her head her 'ski slope', trying to make the boys and me laugh, but we were very frightened – more, I think, because she had no hair when she first came home, than because of the scar which ran jaggedly from about three inches above her right ear, all the way round to the other side. 'You'll think twice before you paint your eggs this Easter,' she'd joked, but we only pretended to laugh.

'Shall I light you a cigarette?' I asked.

'Yes please, baby,' she said. Once again I guided the lit cigarette to her lips.

'Can you feel your legs yet, Mum?'

'Sometimes it feels as if I'm going to move them; but the feeling *will* come back, I'm sure.'

'Mr Bennet is coming from the hospital this afternoon, so maybe we'll know more then,' I suggested. My mother was wearing a pink, silky sleeveless nightie, and now she shivered. 'Are you cold, Mummy?' I asked her.

'A bit, darling,' she said.

'I'll get you a cardigan.' I stubbed out her cigarette.

'I think the blue bed jacket Auntie Ruth knitted me is here somewhere.'

It was lying on the end of the bed. I put it around her shoulders, and as I did so, she pulled me down towards her, running her hands over my face as if to make a mental note of what I looked like; then, cupping my hands round her face, she said, 'Oh God, I love you – Go and help Granny with the shopping, darling, will you?'

'Yes, Mum. Do you want a b – ' I nearly said 'book'. She knew, but she said, 'Bed? Yes, I'd love a bed, this thing's so uncomfortable. Still, 'when our ship comes in', as your Granny says.'

I left her room. Gran was pulling the draw-string on the washing bag that went to the bag-wash every other day. 'Come on, darling,' she said. 'We've been given our orders by the "Above". Take these up on the old push-chair, and I'll be finished here when you get back. We've got a lot more to do.'

I came back from the laundry and put the ticket on the table. Gran was still muttering. ' . . . Expecting me to run here, there and everywhere, like a two-year-old – we've got to go up to the town. I told him. "I'm nearly seventy, you know, Terry." (Gran had always been nearly seventy.) She pulled on her black coat which she wore both summer and winter, and pulled up her wrinkled lisle stocking, tightening the piece of string which was her 'garter'. (Mummy used to laugh and call her eccentric, and when asked whether that meant nice or not, she'd always reply 'nicely odd!')

We got on the first bus, which was followed by another two; they all went to the main shopping area. When we got off the bus, I held Gran's hand and asked, 'What have we got to get now?'

'Oh,' said Gran, 'I've got to see if we've got enough left on the Provident cheque for new sheets and a bolster case, two pillow cases and a nightdress and towel.'

We walked into one of the big department stores, and Gran licked the end of a pencil stub as she added up the prices of the sheets, bolster case, pillow cases and towel; there was a mauve line on her bottom lip from the pencil. She went over the sum about six times before it twice added up to the right figure.

'Here you are, darling, check this over for Granny. You're the Grammar School girl.'

I was hopeless at maths, but made it come to the same amount as Gran had. 'There's one and ninepence over.'

A lady in black came over to us and asked, 'Can I help you, madam?' Gran gave her the list of purchases already selected. 'And I'll take a white flannel with the blue trim,' she added. The items were parcelled up as Gran went around the store, examining various linens.

'Cash or cheque, madam?' asked the assistant in black.

'This,' said Gran, handing over the Provident Cheque with a look of disdain which was only equalled by the stare of the assistant as she received it.

'That will be tuppence to pay, madam.' Gran handed over the two pennies, then, with her head held high, she walked out of the linen department with me following.

'Gran!' I was having trouble keeping up with her now. 'Gran! Your stocking's come down.'

She put the parcel on the floor, bent down, hoisted the stocking above her thin, pale knee, and retied the string. I wanted the ground to swallow me up!

'We haven't got a nightdress,' I hissed.

'I know,' said Gran. 'We're going to Auntie Ruth's house now. She'll give her sister some decent bits. Your aunt lives how she was brought up, like a lady, not the hand-to-mouth way her poor young sister has to. She won't come and see your mother while *he's* there, and I can't say I blame her.'

I had only been to my aunt's house two or three times before, and always to borrow money for my mother. I could never quite work out, when I remembered going into what she called her 'lounge', whether it had an off-white carpet and two white Persian cats, or a white carpet and two off-white cats. I know all the furniture was dark, with gold bits, and we sat on a dusky-pink velvet settee with its end missing.

'Well, what brings you two, Mother?' asked Auntie Ruth. She was seemingly never pleased to see anyone except the cats, of which she made a great fuss the whole of the time she was conversing with you. Whether she had absorbed any of what you had said was never clear. She looked very much like my mother.

'It's your sister, Ruth,' said Gran.

'What seems to be the problem?' she asked, bending down to inspect one cat's ear, while stroking the other cat's ears back.

'She's gone blind.'

'Oh my God!' said Auntie Ruth, suddenly alert.

'No, Granny, no it *will* come back, the doctor's coming from the hospital this afternoon.' The word 'blind' had horrified me, and I'd started to cry.

'Come into the garden, darling,' Gran told me. We walked through long, open glass doors into a garden that looked like something from a picture book. There was a little wooden house, fixed on a long wooden pole; birds were flying on and off the house, and there were red roses and pink carnations. It was a riot of colour. I sat on a wooden seat, and Auntie Ruth brought out a tray with a glass of lemonade and some chocolate biscuits. Then she went in again. After about twenty minutes she came out to the garden, and with some pliers snipped off about a dozen red roses.

'Come along, darling,' she said. 'I've a cab on its way for you and Grandma. You really must try to be a brave girl.' She pressed a bank note into my hand. I hoped it was a pound – if Uncle Alan had been at home, it *would* have been, but I thought it would be impolite to look. It was probably ten shillings. She wrapped the roses in tissue paper, then hurriedly escorted me out; I had a Harrods bag in one hand and the parcel we'd just bought in the other.

'Give Mummy my fondest love, and Uncle Alan's too,' said Auntie Ruth. She quickly put us into the waiting cab, gave directions to the driver, and off we went.

'I've got to telephone her tonight to tell her what the doctor has said,' Gran told me. 'Now the way your Auntie Ruth lives is the way your mother was brought up, and just look at what's happened to her.' (Gran always managed to omit the fact that it was her squandering of the family riches on my mother's side of the family that had ultimately led my mother to her present plight.) As we alighted from the taxi, I noticed that Gran's eyes looked red and puffy, and she was very flushed. I'd never seen Gran cry before, and I was very much disturbed.

We entered the house with our parcels and my father seemed pleased with our purchases, but a momentary frown showed his feelings about our trip to Auntie Ruth's house. He asked Gran and me not to say that Mummy's sister had sent the flowers; I readily agreed, and as he slipped the Players across to Gran, she shrugged and said, 'Why not? If it's going to make her happy to believe that they came from you.' Gran could be quite shrewd – sometimes.

The fish and chips that he must have fetched for Gran and myself had dried up in the oven, but they tasted good. We all went into the bedroom with the parcels, and as I unwrapped the cellophane from the bed linen, my father and Gran began rolling my mother on to one side, so that they could put the bottom sheet under her, and then the top sheet over her. I put the clean pillow cases, which felt like crisp paper, on to the pillows, but had to have help to put the cover on the bolster, because it was too big and awkward. The shape of the bed-settee didn't allow room for the sheets to be tucked in, but they all looked snow-white, and with the eiderdown showing its cleaner patchwork side, it all looked very smart.

Auntie Ruth had sent some pyjamas, one pair white, with faded blue flowers, and the other pair a pale mauve – but the two nighties were the prettiest. One of them was pink, with a mandarin collar and three-quarter sleeves, and the second one was also pink, with lace of the same shade of pink around the V neck.

'Oh Mummy, look!' I said. 'Wear the one with the Chinese collar, it's so pretty.'

Then my hand went over my mouth, and I ran from the room, crying. I just could not, and would not, believe that she couldn't see that nightdress. I went to the scullery to wash the dinner plates that Gran and I had used, and I put the kettle on and made a pot of tea. My father came to stand behind me, and said, 'Here, darlin'.' He held me close. 'Mummy understands yer don't mean things to hurt her. Now, yer go and see yer Mammy. Yer were right, sure she's as pretty as a picture in the nightie yer said to wear. I'll make the tea, yer go in an' see her before the specialist comes.'

'Will he take her back to hospital?' I asked.

'No, darlin', not as long as I've breath in my body, she won't be goin' back to that place,' he said emphatically.

She did indeed look beautiful, with her dark curls against the snowy white pillows, and wearing the high-necked pink gown, she was my real life Jean Simmons, and I loved her so much.

'Now look at this,' said Gran, holding up a large amber-coloured bottle. 'It's French cologne from your sister. And these vests and knickers have never been worn. She's a good girl, is Ruth.'

Just then my father came into the room with the silver tray, on which was a cup of tea and the large bouquet of red roses in a cut-glass bowl.

'Oh Terry, I can smell roses,' cried my mother. He placed the flowers on the oak trolley next to her bed.

'And I expect yer'll be wondering what colour they are, sweetheart?'

'No, Terence,' she said, feeling the smooth petals at her fingertips. 'I can almost see them, and they're red.'

'*Can* you almost see them, Mummy?' I asked, taking her seriously.

'I still have my mind's eye, baby,' she smiled.

'Now if yer'll go and drink yer tea, darlin',' he said to me, 'we're just about ready for this "big white chief", and it'll soon be time then for yer to go and get the baby.' He held out half a crown, and went on, 'If yer could meet the little lads from school, buy yerself an' them all an ice-cream.'

3

As I made my way through the labyrinth of streets to collect Anna, I realized that I hadn't asked how much the boys knew about Mum's sight and the problems with her legs. I hadn't seen any of them that morning. What if they asked? I'd just have to tell them that a doctor was coming, and hope that they wouldn't talk too much about things to Mum.

Anna toddled out from the Wendy house, and her face lit up as she saw me. As I brought her coat from the peg, I realized that I hadn't brought her pushchair, and I was just too weary to carry her all the way back, so I felt in my blazer pocket for the half-crown and walked to the bus stop. Then we only had a short walk through the park to the boys' school, where I saw them across the road with some of their mates, and called to them. I checked for traffic both ways, then they all ran across the road.

'What's happened?' James asked.

'Nothing much. Well, at least, Mummy's still not very well, but a specialist is coming to see her – he'll have been there by now. She's OK though, you know – laughing and things.'

'What's *he* like?' asked Patrick.

'Oh, he's fine.'

'Yeah, he was this morning,' added James. 'Doesn't mean he's gonna be able to keep it up for long though.'

'I hate him,' said Patrick. 'I heard him last night, and what he said to you and Mum.'

'I called to you when it was all happening,' said James, indignantly. 'I must have called you a thousand times, but you didn't answer me once.'

'A thousand times?' asked Patrick, scornfully. 'That would've taken you all night!'

'You're "yella" you are,' shouted James. 'Yella belly, Yella belly, Yella belly!'

Tim joined in, and even Anna attempted the chant. Patrick swung out at James and caught him in the chest.

'Bloody well stop it, you lot!' I yelled. 'Listen, I've pretended to be asleep when I've heard him having a go at Mummy, and I've called you two but you've been "soundo". Anyway, Mum says he's sorry, and he's not going drinking again, and we're all to forget last night. When Mum's better, we're all going for a holiday to Brighton for a week.'

'When?' they asked in unison.

'I told you, when Mummy gets better.'

'I bet he told you that,' said James.

'No, he didn't, clever clogs, Mummy did.'

'Where's Brighton?' asked Tim.

'It's the seaside, Tim,' I told him, 'and Mummy says it's much better than Southend. Anyway, you've all got to be good tonight, because he's bought a load of food and sheets and pillow cases, and loads of other things.'

'And toys?' asked Tim.

'No Tim – but he gave me the money to buy us all a lolly.'

We stopped outside Forrester's newsagents, and bought four lollies and an ice-cream cornet for Anna. As I felt in my pocket for the two shilling piece to pay for them, I felt a piece of squared parchment. It was the money from Auntie Ruth. I took it out of my pocket and saw that it wasn't ten shillings, it was a pound note!

'Hold on to the baby's hand, Jimmy,' I said, as we got outside. 'I won't be a tick.' I bought the *Beano*, *Dandy* and *Topper* for the boys, *Playhour* and *Girl* for Anna and me, and a bottle of cream soda and a box of chocolate gingers for Mummy and Gran.

'Won the Pools, have you?' enquired Mr Forrester.

'No, my Auntie Ruth gave me some money today.'

He looked dubiously at me over his glasses.

'You can ask my Gran, if you like,' I said indignantly, as he handed me the change. Outside the shop the boys stared. 'We had to go to Auntie Ruth's today,' I explained. 'She gave me ten shillings. I only just felt it in my pocket now.'

'You mean you forgot you had a ten bob note?' asked James.

'Jimmy, if you knew the sort of day I've had, you'd have forgotten your bloody head,' I told him. I raked about in my pocket and found another one and sixpence, apart from the remaining ten shilling note. 'Here you are, a tanner each, and you can each buy a sixpenny Walls brick tonight, and we'll make ice-cream sodas.'

'Hey, thanks Sis,' said James.

'Yeah, thanks,' added Patrick.

'Caroline, what's the special thing Mummy's seeing this afternoon?'

'Oh Timmy, it's a special doctor to make her better,' I laughed.

When we arrived home, at about half past four, the table was laid with sandwiches, tinned peaches in a bowl and evaporated milk, which we called cream, and there were chocolate eclairs on a large plate.

Gran came in from the hallway as we all filed in. Her face was even more flushed than it had been that morning, and her eyes were bloodshot. I didn't like this. Gran was old; Linda Payne's Gran had died in her sleep only last week, and Granny was older than her.

'Are you all right, Gran?' I asked.

'Yes, darling, I've just got a head-cold starting.' She sniffed to emphasize the point.

'It's a lovely tea, Gran,' said James.

'Yeah,' echoed the other two, 'it's a lovely tea.' 'Dyaa . . .' came yet another echo, from Anna; we all looked at her and laughed. It was her cue to show off, and for days afterwards she practised the slang 'Yeah'.

'Has the specialist doctor been to see Mummy, Gran?'

'Yes, darling.'

'Is he going to make her better?'

'He's going to try.'

'Can we go in and see her after tea?'

'When she wakes up. Now eat up all those crusts.'

Anna was fishing around in her bowl for the slippery peaches, and she yelled when Gran tried to break them up for her.

'Where's Dad?' asked James. 'Down to the boozer for his afternoon tea?'

'Sshh, Jimmy,' I said.

'He's having a lie down, he's got a lot of pain,' explained Gran.

James, who was still laughing at his previous joke, quipped, 'He *is* a lot of pain!'

'That's enough, Jimmy,' I hadn't heard Gran tell us off before, however bad we'd been — something about her was different. It was her voice, which sounded as if she'd got a bad throat.

'Sit here, Gran,' I said, getting up.

'No, I've got to keep going, my girl.' She sighed deeply.

They were all eating their chocolate eclairs, and Anna was in a dreadful mess.

'Have you got enough cigarettes, Gran?' James asked, suddenly sobered.

'Yes, I've got more today than I usually have in a week. It's all or nothing.'

I cleaned Anna up as best I could, and put the *Playhour* comic on her high chair while I cleared the table. Then I washed up, while James wiped the dishes and Patrick put them away. Timmy made an attempt at wiping the table down. And then suddenly they'd made their way off to the bedroom, leaving Anna yelling to be lifted out of her high chair. I set Mummy and Dad's food to one side, and Gran accepted a cup of tea. She didn't want to eat. I washed the high chair down, and swept under the table with the dustpan and brush.

Someone knocked on the front door, and James went to answer it. I recognized Nurse Parker's voice. 'Well, what a handsome trio you are,' I heard her say to the boys. I put the kettle on to boil.

The nurse bustled into the kitchen. 'Hello, Granny, hello Caroline – oh my, is this the baby?' Anna looked hesitantly at her, and then smiled. 'What a beautiful little girl.' Anna had recognized someone who might release her from the bondage of the high chair, and held her arms outstretched. 'Just a moment, darling, Nursie has to go and get lots of things from the car, and then she'll give you cuddles.' With that, she came back from the car carrying armfuls of sheets, red rubber ones, white ones, jars and tins.

'Is there anywhere we can keep these things, Granny?' she asked.

'The very top of that cupboard,' said Gran, opening the door. Her voice had definitely changed since this morning. I even wondered if I should mention it to the nurse, but decided against that. I brought a chair, and the nurse began stacking some of the white sheets and the red rubber ones in a neat pile.

'We bought new sheets this morning, Nurse,' I said.

'Yes, sweetheart, but you can never have enough,' she said. She put the pile of white sheets and red rubber sheets on the back of the chair; the bottles, tins and jars were now on the kitchen table in a metal tray affair.

'I've just made some tea. Would you like some, Nurse?'

'That would be lovely. And it looks as if Granny should have a cup too.'

She had picked Anna out of the high chair. 'Well, how you've grown! You look just like your sister, you really do,' she cried. Anna had been showing her a doggy on a piece of her comic which she'd already torn, and now the baby wriggled down and went in the direction of the hallway.

'She'll wake Mummy,' I said.

'Well, I peeped in a minute ago, and your Mummy was awake, sweetheart.' Nurse Parker went into the scullery and I heard her fill the kettle. 'Perhaps you'd like to take a cup of tea in to your mum, while I drink mine and wait for the kettle to boil.'

I quickly poured the tea, and took it into the front room.

'Hello Mum, what did the special doctor say?'

'Oh, he seems to think it will all right itself in time, and it's one of those things that happens. He seemed to agree with my theory that the epilepsy could also be part of it — we've just got to be patient, darling. Now, did I hear the patter of tiny feet in the hall just now?'

'It's Anna. She's torn her comic, and I expect she's about to start on the others. Nurse Parker wants to see to you, and then we'll all come in.'

'Yes please, darling. Is Daddy in the kitchen?'

'No,' I said, 'he's having a snooze, but he won't sleep for long with the noise they're making.'

Nurse Parker came in, carrying the sheets over her arm and a big enamel jug of water in one hand. She put the jug on the floor and the sheets on the sideboard, then went to fetch two metal bowls and her tray of bottles and jars. There was also an enormous blue-wrapped roll of cotton wool.

'I've put the kettle back on', she said to me, 'so that you can give Anna a wash. Granny tells me she likes you to wash her.'

'Caroline makes bubbles for her and I can't,' said Mum.

I left the room, and found Anna's pyjamas, nappy, vest and rubbers on the fireguard. Her soap, flannel and zinc powder were laid out on a nappy on the kitchen table.

'Take her out, will you,' growled Patrick. I washed the basin out with Oxydol and a little of the water from the kettle, then filled the basin with warm water. Anna had hollered the whole time. Gran still sat at the kitchen table, her hands round the teacup, and not even smoking! I would mention it to the nurse, I thought. Anna sat in the warm water, splashing around. I washed her all over and she screamed as I took her out of the water; then I dried her, powdered her and dressed her, all in record time. She leapt from my lap, and dived for the door, to get back to the boys, so I ran after her and called the boys to come through and bring their pyjamas.

'Right, who's dirtiest?' I asked. It was Tim. 'Right, you first, then Jimmy.'

'Don't be so bloody bossy!'

'I'm not. Mum wants to see us all for a while after the nurse has gone.'

'Well, you usually are.' James always had to have the last word. I helped Timmy to get the worst of the dirt off, and put his pyjamas on, then Nurse Parker came through with her jug and bowls.

'Can you pop in and say goodnight to Irene, Granny?' she asked.

Gran got up slowly. I watched from the scullery door as Nurse Parker emptied the two bowls, swilled them round with the water from the jug, dried them both with a pad of cotton wool, and asked where she could leave them.

'There might be room enough under here,' I said, and pulled back the curtain that was tacked around the sink. We managed to squeeze the bowls into a corner. 'Right, I'll see you all tomorrow night,' she said, putting on her navy blue mac, which she'd left draped across Mummy's white-winged rocking chair.

'Tell Granny I'm just going, will you, Caroline?'

I went into the front room. Gran was sitting on a chair next to the bed-settee, holding Mum's hand, and my father was sitting on the side of the bed.

'Nurse is going, Gran,' I said. Gran bent to kiss my mother goodnight, and my mother said, 'Goodnight Mum, God bless. Try and get an early night, and thanks for everything.'

Gran even bent to kiss my father. This was something I'd never seen happen before, and it seemed as if the whole world was going crazy. Gran followed me out and collected her coat and bag, then kissed us all, holding us too tightly, as usual.

'Nurse is giving me a lift to Auntie Ruth's,' she explained. 'But I'll be back at seven in the morning as usual. Goodnight, darlings.'

'Goodnight you kids,' added Nurse Parker. 'Not too late to bed now – nurse's orders,' she laughed.

'Goodnight, Nurse,' we called, 'Goodnight Gran.'

'Come on you lot,' I said. 'It's eight o'clock, and you haven't seen Mummy.'

We headed for the front room. Dad was holding her hand, and he looked very grey and old.

23

'Here's our chilluns, sweetheart,' he told her.

'Come and give your mummy big kisses,' she said. One by one the others made their way over to the bed and kissed their mother. I hung back till last, when Anna decided to snuggle in beside her, while the boys tried to outdo each other with tales of their day. James said he liked her new nightie, Patrick called him a creep, and Timmy tried to tell a joke of which he could not remember the ending.

'Sing "Ugly Duckling" Mum,' said little Timmy.

'All right then – ready? "There once was an ugly duckling, with feathers all stubby and brown . . . and the other birds, in so many words, said . . . ," ' Here we all made the appropriate noises until the song had finished, going on to 'I'm a pink toothbrush, you're a blue toothbrush'.

'Say the "Nurse's Pins" for us, Mummy,' said little Timmy.

'All right,' she laughed, 'but then it's bed for all of you.'

Dad looked on, smiling and somehow fascinated, as she began:

'A kiss when I wake in the morning,
A kiss when I go to bed,
A kiss when I cut my finger,
A kiss when I bump my head.
A kiss when my bath is over,
A kiss when my bath begins:
Our Mummy's as full of kisses
As our Nanny's full of pins!

'Can I have that kiss when you go to bed now?' We all laughed and kissed her and Daddy 'goodnight'. Anna had fallen asleep beside her; I was about to carry the baby to her cot when my mother felt my arm and held it.

'Leave her here for a little while, darling. Daddy will take her in.'

The whole time we'd been with her, Mum's face had been turned towards us, but her eyes were not actually on any of us, though the boys had noticed nothing untoward. I felt suddenly terribly alone. I made ice-cream soda for the boys and went to bed.

4

The next two or three days followed in a similar way. Granny was always there in the mornings. Our white plimsolls and Anna's sandals would be cleaned with the round block of whitener and left to dry on the window-sill in the sun. Dad had put the wireless in the front room for Mummy to listen to.

Sometimes, if we were alone, I'd ask her about her sight, but eventually I didn't ask any more. Her many friends would come in, and although nothing was said, my father would stay in the kitchen until they'd gone. I'd been told that if anyone asked, I was to say that Mummy had temporary trouble with her sight, and the boys were to say the same thing.

One morning my father came into the kitchen, holding a letter. 'Come on, chilluns,' he said. 'I want yer to come into Mammy's room. I've some news for us all.'

We all followed him in, and he started to read the letter. It was from the Royal Navy, expressing regret at the loss of the tops of three of his fingers. (We'd forgotten about this, though it had been very traumatic at the time, and had grown used to the two nail-less stumps and the little finger that bore an ugly, twisted piece of nail.)

' . . . and so, if you agree to the sum written on the enclosed cheque, please sign . . . you have the right to appeal . . . '

'How much is it, Terence?' Foolishly, he held the paper in front of her eyes, then quickly withdrew it, realizing what he'd done.

'Five pounds,' he said. Then, 'Just a minute, it's got one five and two noughts.'

'But that's five hundred, Terence!' Mum exclaimed.

'Of course it is, darlin', I was just jestin' with yers.'

'We're rich! we're rich! we're rich!' we all squealed, dancing around the room.

Over the next three weeks my father bought new saucepans, plates, blankets, sheets, clothes; a new bed was brought through for my mother, and he rearranged the front room to accommodate that, and had curtains made in 'Old Gold', with a matching bedspread. I'd had my summer uniform (which was compulsory) at last, but he'd forgotten to buy the straw hat. I couldn't ask him for one, but was acutely aware of being the only girl in full summer uniform – with the winter beret. The final purchase was the biggest surprise to us all – a twenty-one inch TV set.

This monstrosity sat on the sideboard, facing my mother, and in the evenings we would watch the 'Grove Family', and adverts for tinned peas that danced, and jams, and soap that all the film stars used. Gran continued to have a bad throat, and was far less talkative. Sometimes Dad would go to his bedroom and lie on the bed, smoking, not seeming to notice me enter or leave the room when I fetched him tea.

Gradually Nurse Parker called more often, and our stays with Mummy, watching television, grew shorter, until eventually they stopped altogether. Now we were only allowed in to kiss her goodnight. But it was summer, and the boys would be out with their friends, and I would take Anna up to the park, to 'tire her out'. She slept with me now, and began to cling to me. Oh, how I hated to leave her at the nursery in the mornings.

New foods came into the house, and a strange cup appeared, with a handle and spout. Dad taught me how to use this, and I would make up a cupful of Brand's Essence of Beef tea and milk for my mother. Her mouth seemed swollen, as I'd coax her to take 'Just a drop more, Mummy.' I would also feed her Bengers' Food and Robinson's Patent Groats. These were more difficult, as it was becoming increasingly hard for her to swallow; her lips and tongue were slimy and white. There was large swelling now where her 'ski slope' was. Gran was beginning to spend the odd day away from the house, and Mum's friends no longer visited, but would leave fresh eggs and flowers for her.

One evening, after Nurse Parker had left (she called frequently now to give my mother her washes, and the tablets had been supplanted by injections), Dad called us all into the kitchen.

'Darlins,' he said, 'I don't know how to make this easy for any of you, but your Mammy isn't going to be with us much longer.'

'Where's she going, back to hospital?' I asked.

'No, my sweet.' His voice was hushed, and tears were beginning to slide onto his cheeks. 'I promised you all I'd never let that happen. No, Mummy's going to Heaven.'

I hated him. How could he be saying this, and frightening us so? Somewhere from my throat a strangled growl asked, 'Are you saying she's going to die?'

'Yes, darlin',' he said, a horrible hooting sound rising from his chest and coming out of his mouth as he dropped his head on to his arms and sobbed. I looked round at the boys. James was the first to move; he darted from the room, looking terrified. Patrick started crying, as did Anna, who was sitting on my lap. I wanted to run away too, but I looked at Tim — a dark patch was growing on his trousers. I took his hand, and left the room.

In the bedroom James was sitting on his bed, staring into his hands; Patrick was lying across the bed, crying, as we entered.

'Jimmy, take the baby,' I said. I knelt and took Timmy's grey trousers and pants off, and put his pyjamas on. Then I quickly undressed Anna, putting a clean nappy and nightie on her.

'I'm going to get the baby a bottle,' I said, handing her back to James.

'Don't be bloody long,' he growled, as Anna started crying again. 'And shut up you,' he poked Patrick in the back.

That evening, after we'd kissed Mummy good night, with the boys looking at her very intently on this occasion, we had a 'meeting'.

'Well, I don't believe him,' said James defiantly. 'He said *he'd* maybe be going to Heaven when he went into hospital. Do you remember? — Well, he bloody didn't and he still kids himself they'd have him there!' James was right, though; our father *had* made a similar speech then.

'Yeah, *and* he asked us to look after Mummy then,' recalled Patrick.

'He frightens me,' said Tim.

'Well, he doesn't frighten me,' I lied, cuddling him.

We all decided that James was right, and Dad was not to be believed; and yet I felt our mother wasn't the same any more, she was changing. I would chatter away as I tried to feed her, but she would only make small grunts and shake her head, and more often than not fall asleep.

The morning after our 'meeting' was a Saturday, and I walked into the front room to see her, not realizing Nurse Parker was there. But it wasn't Nurse Parker's presence that made me run from that room. Mummy was lying on her right-hand side, and there was a large dark red hole, bigger than my hand, at the bottom of her spine.

Early on the Sunday afternoon Auntie Ruth and Uncle Alan called. They stayed a short time with Mummy and then came out into the kitchen as we were finishing lunch. Gran wasn't coming until later in the afternoon, and I'd put Dad's dinner in the oven. He didn't eat very often now. He came in with our visitors, and I could see that Auntie Ruth had been crying. Uncle Alan was lovely to us all, and insisted that he would wash up while I made a cup of tea.

They stayed for tea. Uncle Alan had brought a bottle of rum with him, bigger than the normal size that Daddy used to buy. 'Thanks, Alan,' Dad said, putting his arm round Uncle Alan's shoulder, 'but I promised them all that I wouldn't again.'

'Do you kids object if your Dad has a drop of this in his tea?' Uncle Alan asked.

'No,' we all said. He filled Dad's cup to the top with the rum, and added some to his own cup, then held out his hand and said, 'Which hand is the lucky one?' After playing this game for some time, he eventually let Anna point, and opened his palm on which rested a large note.

'It's a fiver!' yelled James.

'Five pounds, darling, not "a fiver" – that's such a common expression,' said Auntie Ruth.

'Sorry,' said James, fearing he'd lose favour – and fearing even more that he would lose the sight of the fiver.

'What do yer say to yer auntie and uncle, chillun?' said Dad.

'Thank you very much,' we chanted, kissing them both.

The following morning Gran hadn't arrived and we were late. Dad was still in bed, and James was irritably trying to shovel cornflakes down Anna's throat as I rushed around, changing for school myself.

'Where's Mummy's beaker?' No one answered. I searched the kitchen cabinet, and eventually made my way into the front room. 'Hello Mummy,' I said. Her mouth opened, but no sound came. The lump on her head was now enormous. I kissed her cheek, but even her skin smelt strange, a sort of acid, woody smell mingled with the sort of smell that's in your mouth and throat after you've had a tooth out. Auntie Ruth's perfume, that Nurse Parker put on Mummy every day, seemed to evaporate within this smell.

I caught sight of her beaker on the window-sill and reached across for it. As I did so, my elbow hit her head. This time an audible moan came from her throat.

'Oh Mummy, I'm sorry,' I said. 'Have I hurt you?' She raised her fingers slightly. 'I'll get you a cup of tea.'

As I was leaving the room, Nurse Parker was coming along from the kitchen, carrying the jug and basins.

'I'm just getting Mummy her tea,' I said. 'We're late this morning. She groaned just now, I think she's in pain, I . . .'

'Listen, you just get yourselves off to school. I'll give Mummy her injection right away, and I'll make her her tea. I usually have a cup with her if I've got time.'

5

During lesson that morning one of the feared Sixth Form girls came in. We all looked up as she spoke to the teacher; then they both looked at me briefly.

'Caroline, go to Dr Barton's office, dear. And don't look so worried.'

'You're for it,' said Patricia Mackie, who sat next to me.

'That's enough, Patricia,' Miss Jones chided. I got up, feeling my face flush, and left the room.

When I knocked on the Head's door, she called out, 'Come!' Timidly I opened her door. I knew I was for it, I'd had to take so much time off school.

'Sit down, my dear.' She spoke quietly, but looked as forbidding as ever in her black gown and half glasses. 'Now, what I'm going to say is in confidence — I mean it is only between you and I, dear. Your teachers and I have been very saddened to hear of your mother's illness — How is she, by the way?'

'They say she's going to die, Madam.' Tears were stinging the back of my nose and throat.

'And you're having to do a great deal of the caring for your younger brothers and sister, I understand?'

'Yes, Madam.'

'Well, my dear, if there is anything the staff and I can do, or if you feel you need to talk to us, please don't be afraid to come to us.' She reached across and squeezed my hand, then quickly withdrew. 'Now, the other thing I wanted to say was that we have certain school funds, limited though they may be, and we are still able to assist girls like yourself . . . I'll come to the point. You don't own the regulation straw hat, do you, dear?'

'No, Madam.'

'Well, out of these funds I have purchased one for you.' She reached behind her back and brought out a school summer hat; even my red house badge had been stitched on.

'Thank you, Madam.' I said, and then the tears began to fall. She stood up and, walking round her desk towards me, put her hands gently on my shoulders.

'Now, my dear, I want you to go to Nurse and ask her to make you a nice cup of tea and let you have a little lie down until lunch break.' Reaching under the folds of her black gown, she extracted a clean white handkerchief and placed it in my hand.

'Thank you, Madam,' I said, as she walked to the door.

The afternoon was scorchingly hot as I made my way home, with Anna on my hip and my satchel weighing heavily on my shoulder to balance up the weight. Anna kept tugging at my new hat. As I walked down the street, a lot of the neighbours were smiling at me, and I guessed it was because I looked so smart now that my summer uniform was complete.

Maggie, a pretty woman with blonde hair, lived in a prefab opposite our flat. She was a widow, and had three girls. 'Caroline!' she called, as I passed the window of Mummy's room, which looked out on to the steet. I saw that Dad had closed the curtains – it must must be baking hot in there. Maggie came across to me. 'I think your Daddy's looking for you. Let me take Anna and give her a drink and a swing.' The baby didn't resist, she liked Maggie and her swing!

I walked through the back door, and called, 'Gran!' There was no answer. My father came to the door, tears flooding his face, a rosary in his hand.

'Darlin', come quickly, come with Daddy.' He pulled me along the passage-way into the front room. My mother was lying with her head a little to one side, mouth slightly open, the tip of her tongue protruded; a thick white substance was covering her lips and tongue, and one side of her mouth was sagging, giving the impression of a sickly leer. Both her arms were at her sides, and her eyes were not quite closed.

'She's gone, darlin', yer Mammy's dead. Kiss her, darlin', an' say "God rest your soul, Mammy".'

This wasn't my mother; this was a monster, a nightmare. I had to get away. 'No!' I screamed. 'I want my Mummy!'

My father gripped my hand tightly, dragging me down to the floor. I tried to get up again, and felt her hand as I gripped the bed for support. The hand was warm.

'Now kiss her.' He was kneeling by me. 'Kiss her and say, "God rest your soul, Mammy".'

'I kissed her hand, and began, 'God rest your – '

'Not her hand. Yer kiss her mouth and say –'

'No!'

'This is yer Mammy, who's spent her life lovin' yer and kissin' yer wid those lips. Now kiss her, yer little bastard!'

I kissed her sticky mouth, my stomach turning. 'God rest your soul, Mum . . . '

A cic . . . cic . . . cic . . . sound came from her throat. 'She's not dead!' I screamed.

'Sure she is.'

I turned to run, but once again he dragged me back across the room. I'd wet my knickers, and the elastic of my hat, which was somewhere at the back of my neck, was round my throat.

'Yer'll say the rosary wid me, sure yer will.'

'Hail Mary, full of grace, the Lord is with thee. Blessed art thou amongst women and blessed is the fruit of thy womb, Jesus. Holy Mary, mother of God, pray for us sinners now and in the hour of our death, Amen. Our Father – '

There was a loud knock on the door. I ran from the room and up the public hallway. I'd glimpsed the long robes of the priest and heard a voice that could only have been Granny screaming 'Irene!' I ran and ran, past the shops, through the park, and up to the boys' school, then up the steps and through the glass door into the headmaster's office. It was empty. I ran into two classrooms before I burst into one where they were saying prayers.

'Mr Wilson, please help me,' I gasped.

'Class dismissed,' he said, and came running to me, hurrying me away from the classroom. 'Tyler!' he called to a passing boy, 'ask Mr Dunne to round up the O'Farrell boys and take them to the staff room. Is that clear?'

'Yes, sir,' said the boy, looking scared.

Mr Wilson took me into his office, but my jumbled words and the terror I'd just lived through didn't seem to be affecting him as I thought it would.

'I don't even think she's dead, Mr Wilson,' I ended. 'She made a funny noise in her throat.'

But Mr Wilson *was* affected. His hand was trembling as he took my hand and prayed for all of us – though I didn't want to hear any more prayers.

'We've got to have strength to tell your brothers, and He will give us that.'

The boys were in the staff room, nibbling on biscuits, and sharing a cup of something. As soon as I saw them I had no strength; I knew that they would share my pain.

'She's dead, boys! Mummy's dead!' I told them. They all looked at Mr Wilson, almost for confirmation. Mr Dunne stood there looking helpless, and James said to Mr Wilson, 'Can we go now, sir?'

'Let me take you.'

'No, sir, it's all right. We've got to get our baby sister, thank you,' I said.

Both teachers saw us down the school steps. Timmy had started to cry, and Patrick was wiping his eyes with the back of his hands. Only James was silent.

'When did she die?' the boys asked.

'I don't know. Just before I got back with Anna.'

'Who told you?'

'Dad. – He made me go and see her.'

'What! When she was dead?'

'Yes.' I started crying, and that set all four of us off. We passed Mr Forrester's sweet shop; I had no money, and Timmy wanted a lolly, but we thought we could ask Mr Forrester if he would let us have one, and we'd bring the money straight back – then James found a sixpence, so we could share one.

(I hadn't had a drink since lunch-time and the sun was still blisteringly hot.) We all wandered into the shop – we seemed afraid to lose sight of each other.

'What's the matter with you lot? Lost a pound and found a penny?' asked Mr Forrester.

'No, our Mummy's just died,' I said, breaking into more tears.

'Oh you poor little buggers,' he said. 'When?'

'Just before I got back from school,' I told him.

'Oh, I *am* sorry. What did you want?'

'Just a lolly, please,' I said.

'Looks like you can all do with one.' He took four lollies and an ice-cream cornet. 'This is for the baby. Can't leave her out. – Well, I never did! They say only the good die young. Lovely woman, your mother.' (This was something we were going to hear constantly over the next few months.) 'Just a minute, you kids,' he added, and he started picking up dolly mixtures, fruit salads and black-jacks, liquorice and sweet lollies, and putting them all in a bag.

'We'll bring you the money.'

'No, this is my treat. Tell your Dad I'll start a collection right away.'

When we reached Maggie's, she told me that Anna and myself were staying the night at her house, while the boys were to go up to the Williams's flat, which cheered them up, as their hero was the eldest boy, Pete Williams. Gran came across to Maggie's with clothes for Anna and myself, and we all cried again, Maggie too. Mrs Williams had arrived, and she was beside herself.

'I just thought it was a bit of a set-back. Oh, she was so good to me,' she wailed. Gran went back to collect all the boys' things, then Maggie made Gran stay for a cup of tea, and we heard how 'Terry' had sent Gran out for the priest, and Gran and the priest had been too late. Dr Scanlon had only just given her an injection, and had been gone only ten minutes when she started breathing strangely. Gran was going to spend the night at Auntie Ruth's, but she'd be back in the morning.

That night, sleeping in the strange bed in the prefab with Anna, I got up and looked at the window opposite, where my mother lay. The light in the room was flickering eerily through the yellow curtains. I called Auntie Maggie and she said Dad had lit candles, and that the Irish did stay with their loved ones through the nights after their death, and I must try to sleep. But I stood at the window, and now and again I would see my father pacing up and down. At last I got into bed beside Anna and cried myself to sleep. All the time the episode in the front room with him kept trying to force itself on me, all the stronger as I tried to push it back. It has never left me.

We spent another two nights at our neighbours' before we set foot inside the flat again. Gran came over each day, and her crying made me absolutely distraught. Auntie Ruth and Uncle Alan came too, and they insisted on giving both Maggie and Mrs Williams some money.

On the Thursday morning we were told that the flat was to be opened so that we could pay our last respects to our mother, before the funeral on Friday morning. When Maggie and Gran eventually got me to go over to the flat, it took some time before I realized why people were queuing right out as far as the entrance of the mansions. Maggie was carrying the baby, and we had to squeeze through to get past the people waiting and the people coming out, so that we could go in through the back way.

Some of the people were Mummy's friends, and they were crying bitterly, murmuring about her being so young and beautiful. I even heard someone say she was like a bride. Some of the people, who were most certainly not her friends, were shuffling through with hankies to the ready; some I'd never seen before in my life, and I wondered if my mother had.

We went into the kitchen. Auntie Ruth was there, with a face like fury.

'Mother! What the hell is he doing? This is the most disgraceful thing I've ever known! It's just a damned pin-to-see-the-peep-show to him. Why doesn't he just go the whole hog and charge admission?'

'Calm down, Ruth, for God's sake,' said Uncle Alan. 'The little ones are here.'

'Why are all the people here, Uncle Alan?' I asked. I was trembling all over.

'Well, darling, they've come to see your Mummy for the last time.'

'You mean they're seeing her dead?'

'Yes, love, and she looks very beautiful.'

'I don't have to see her, do I?' I begged.

'Well, your Daddy will want you to.'

'But I've seen her, and she's horrible!' I couldn't control my trembling.

'When did you see her?' asked Auntie Ruth.

'When she'd just died. He made me kiss her, and her mouth was all open and . . .'

'Oh my God, Alan,' cried my aunt, 'he's insane! This poor child – he's done *that* to her? Well, I'm sorry, but I want a word with him!'

She walked out of the room. Mrs Williams came in next, with the boys, then Auntie Ruth came back. 'He's asking the 'ghouls' to come back in half an hour, as he'd like the close family to see her. I'm surprised he's remembered she had any.' The boys went in with Auntie Ruth, Uncle Alan and Mrs Williams, while Maggie stayed with me and Anna. Uncle Alan's sudden reappearance startled me. I thought it was my father coming to drag me in again.

'Look darling,' said Uncle Alan, 'I think you should come and see her, for your own sake. She looks like a fairy princess, and it will take away those terrible memories.'

Maggie got up, handing Anna back to me. I didn't care if he killed me, I would not go and see her. Then Maggie came back with James.

'Tell your sister what Mummy looks like, Jimmy,' she said.

'She's pretty,' he said.

Eventually Uncle Alan took my hand and Maggie held Anna's and James's hands. I kept my eyes shut tight all the way through the hall and into the room. The overpowering smell of flowers took my breath away, and when I opened my eyes, wreaths were everywhere, She wasn't in the bed by the window. That had gone. In the middle of the room, on a long wooden table thing, there was a light-coloured wooden coffin, and as I approached, I saw that there were angels in gold around the coffin. The rim of the coffin was trimmed with lace, and inside it was lined with satin.

She lay on a satin pillow, and wore the most beautiful 'dress' I had ever seen. It had a slight V-shaped neck, trimmed with lace, and reached down to her feet, where you could just see white satin shoes. The sleeves were wide and trimmed with the same lace, and her hands were crossed and her fingernails painted (something she had never done). Her face was like a doll's, with pink cheeks and lips, and her black lashes curled upwards; her short black curls were arranged prettily, and covered the massive lump – or had it gone? There were clusters of tiny white rosebuds.

I looked at her face, my eyes glancing only once at the rosary she held, together with a single red rose. Uncle Alan squeezed my hand, and I saw his cheeks were wet. He bent and kissed her lips, and had to lift me up to kiss her. Then one by one, the boys were lifted up and kissed her. Maggie lifted the baby up, and she said, pointing a chubby finger, 'Mummy!' Auntie Ruth had her arms around Granny, and they were rocking gently.

I looked at my father. He too was swaying slightly, but his eyes were dry. He smiled. 'Isn't she beautiful, chilluns?' he asked. We nodded.

The boys looked at her once more, and Mrs Williams bent to kiss her as she led them out. So did Maggie, this time telling Anna to kiss Mummy, which she managed to do. Uncle Alan kissed my hand and squeezed it as we made to go. Then I suddenly ran back, and kissed her three times on the lips. 'You're much more beautiful than Jean Simmons, Mummy,' I whispered to myself. 'You're my beautiful Mummy in a box.'

'Terence,' said Auntie Ruth, 'the children aren't going tomorrow.'

'We'll see,' he said.

'No, Terence, they're not.'

The next morning Auntie Ruth had her way, and as the four black Rolls Royces drove slowly around the block, the streets lined with friends and neighbours, the men with heads bowed and hats removed, I watched from Maggie's garden. All the cars were heavily laden with flowers. Gran was with Dad, Auntie Ruth and Uncle Alan in the first car, and every now and then Gran would give a beckoning 'royal wave' to the crowds, until my father's bony hand stretched across and pulled the blind down. How my mother would have laughed at that!

As the cars came round for the third time, and turned left, indicating that they would not be coming around again, I strained my eyes and fixed them on the coffin until the last pinpoint of brown wood disappeared, and I said out loud, 'Mummy, I'll never see you again.'

'That's where you're wrong, my sweetheart,' said Maggie's mother, her arms wrapped around me. 'One day you'll meet again, in 'eaven, or don't you believe in a 'eaven?'

'No, I don't,' I replied, and took Anna, and put her on the swing.

6

The following weeks were part of the school holidays, and we were back home again now. Granny had become a rather sad person. Her eccentric ways, described by Mummy as 'nicely odd' had become just 'decidedly odd'. Although her great affection for us never waned, we had to accept that some mornings she wouldn't show up; but this didn't disturb us unduly, as there were many of my mother's friends who would include us in their own trips to Regent's Park Zoo and Battersea Fun-fair whilst we were in our newly acquired 'motherless' state.

My father would frequently spend days out at the cemetery, but there was always someone to give us a snack or let us come in to play when we reported 'no one's in'. Auntie Ruth came once on her own and took us to buy some summer clothes. (It was during these holidays that another bombshell was to fall, when we heard that Uncle Alan had suffered a heart attack.)

One day I plucked up courage and asked Dad if some of our friends could come in and watch the TV. Since I had only one friend, Gina, and the boys had many, Dad didn't seem to mind, and even laid on crisps and Tizer. The kids were obviously awed by the sight of the huge TV screen (they had none of them believed it possible that you could get a TV set with a screen that size), and it seemed to please Dad immensely when Roy Barnes remarked, 'It makes ours look like peeping through a bloody keyhole!' Dad was obviously drinking again, but he was kind to us.

One morning Gran turned up early and was taking the sheets off the beds, which had been sadly neglected, as well as collecting the towels which had begun to smell sour and were stiff with dirt. She was bagging these things up, and I was waiting to take them to the bag-wash. Gran had already put the second line of clothes out, and she had hung one of Mum's 'new' towels behind the door. Dad came in, bleary-eyed, and after I had quickly made his tea and gone back to waiting for any more bits to be added to the top of the already over-filled bag, he sauntered out to the scullery to shave.

What occurred next happened so quickly that it was hard to absorb.

'And who, in God's name, gave yer the right to hang one of *her* towels behind this door for any Tom, Dick or Harry to wipe their filthy hands or worse on?' he yelled. It was directed at me, but my grandmother hastily owned up to being the culprit.

'There's no living soul in this world who's fit to touch anything of hers,' he ranted. Gran looked frightened, but stood up to him. 'I hope you include yourself with the rest of the world, Terence,' she said, and took the offending towel from the hook and refolded it, folding it over and over again.

Suddenly he moved so swiftly that I thought he would hit her. Instead, he snatched the towel from her hands and screamed, 'It most definitely means you, yer feckin' ole biddy!' Anna was screaming too, and swiftly Gran grabbed the washing bag, picked up Anna and her handbag, and saying quietly to me, 'Come on, darling,' she led us out through the back yard and the outer hallway into the streets. As we passed the bomb-site where the boys were playing, Gran called across to them, 'Meet us in the park at twelve o'clock, boys, and try not to get any dirtier.'

On the way to the laundry Gran didn't speak, and I could think of nothing to say. On the way back she sent me into Forrester's for ten Woodbines, dolly mixtures for the baby and some black-jacks for myself. When I came out of the shop, Gran was talking to Mrs Tyler, who insisted we go back with her for a cup of tea. I left the push-chair outside Mrs Tyler's house, and was told to take Anna out into the little garden to show her the Tyler rabbits in their cages.

As we were leaving, Mrs Tyler told Gran to come back and see her, and to stand up to *him* whatever happened. 'That's what comes of getting involved with a bloody foreigner like 'im,' she said. 'I never could understand what your girl saw in 'im, apart from 'is looks and his swaggering ways. I only hope for your sake, gal, none of it comes out in these young 'uns.'

This left me worrying, and wondering if there was something we hadn't been told about that could come out in us. While I waited for Granny to come out of the fish and chip shop, I examined my bare arms and feet. When we went up to the old churchyard with our fish and chips, we found the boys sliding down a shiny, sloping gravestone. They came running over when they saw us, and began swooping down on the chips while I fed Anna (and myself) bits that hadn't yet managed to become grey from the boys' hands. Then we had a drink from the fountain of drinking water in the park, while Anna drained the last of the orange juice from her bottle.

It was a stifling hot day, and when we got back, laden with the cleaned linen, Gran remained out in the yard, taking down the clean washing from the clothes line, and pegging out the sheets and pillow cases from the washing bag. I hung about, not wanting to go in, but Anna was rubbing her eyes as I carried her through the front door.

There was a pretty young lady sitting at the kitchen table; she had obviously been watching us through the kitchen window, while Dad had been sitting with his back to us. Some photographs of us children, and one with him and Mummy, were on the table.

'You must be Caroline,' said the pretty young lady, holding out her hand to me. I shook it hard as my father always insisted we did. (A limp handshake was a sign of a weak and insincere character — but I often wonder how many would-be foster parents in the years to come misinterpreted the vice-like grip I extended to them, leaving them wincing at a sign of latent aggression.)

'Darlin', this is Miss Bowden.'

'Hello,' I said, shyly.

'And this must be Anna,' said the young lady. She went to hold the baby's hand, but Anna put her hand round my neck and buried her face in my chest.

'She's tired,' I explained. I found a bottle and started to attempt to pour some milk into the narrow-necked glass. Dad quickly jumped up and finished the job for me, but gave up on trying to pull the teat over the top.

'Let me,' offered Miss Bowden, jumping up; she had nearly as much difficulty as he did, but was eventually successful.

My father knocked on the window, through which Gran could be seen just staring vaguely at a white sheet, turning dolly pegs round and round in her hands.

'Come in, Mother, and have a cup of tea, for goodness sake.' When she came in, Gran was wearing her Queen Victoria face. 'Miss Bowden, I want you to meet my mother-in-law. Mother, this is Miss Bowden from the Welfare Offices.'

'Pleased to meet you,' said Gran stiffly, ignoring the pretty girl's proffered hand.

'... and you, Mrs ... uh ... ?'

'Gran will do, that's what everyone calls me — or at least they did until this morning!' She shot Dad a meaningful look, and there was an awkward silence.

'I'll take the baby and get her off,' I said.

I laid myself down beside Anna, and was only half-way through 'Ma Curly Headed Babby', a song that Mummy had sung to all of us, when Anna was asleep. I left her on the bed, and went into the front bedroom. The cot had been dismantled (it was later to be broken up by my father in one of his rages, and used for firewood). I stood in front of the wardrobe mirror, and lifted up my blouse. My nipples had begun to feel bruised, and although they were slightly swollen, they weren't big like those of some of the girls at school. I also looked under my arms for any sign of hair growing, and with shock (mingled with pleasure) I detected the fine growth of four or five hairs under one arm and two under the other. Ashamed, I quickly pulled my blouse down.

My mother's dresses and two coats were hanging in the wardrobe, and there were also various pairs of shoes. I touched every dress and coat. In a box at the bottom was a hat box. It was round and striped, and contained some scarves, letters, two empty dark-blue bottles of 'Evening in Paris', the large bottle of French cologne that Auntie Ruth had given Mum, with only about an inch left in the bottom, a couple of brooches, one of which had lost its pin, a black rosary and two odd earrings. I selected a pink chiffon scarf and the bottle of cologne, then, quietly shutting the wardrobe door, I crept from the room with my 'bounty' and into the bedroom where Anna was sleeping. Quietly too, I opened the bottom drawer that Anna and I shared, hid the bottle of cologne, and put the chiffon scarf under the newspaper that lined the drawer.

Anna was fast asleep, and I went back into the kitchen. Miss Bowden was just leaving, and judging from the full ash-tray and Gran's more relaxed mood, I guessed that she and Dad had 'made up'.

Two days later there was a knock on the door, just as the signature tune for 'Housewives' Choice' was drifting through the house; I'd been trying to figure out how the Puffed Wheat packet could seriously be believed when it said 'Shot from Guns'. James ran to answer the knock, and a plump, jolly lady came in, announcing that she was Mrs Quincy and had come to 'do' for us. As August drew to its close, Mrs Quincy was as good as her word: she certainly did 'do' for us. Beds were made, floors scrubbed and polished, the only carpet (in the front room) was swept with the battered cleaner, and windows were washed.

Mrs Quincy had become a great ally for Gran, and they spent their 'cuppa' times talking about the War and rationing, and Mummy and Auntie Ruth when they were children, and the big house they had lived in and the maids they had had. Sometimes they'd take turns with the ironing, and it wasn't beneath Mrs Quincy to put the bag-wash on the push-chair and get a bit of shopping too. This left less for all of us to do. Sometimes I'd walk into the kitchen when Granny and Mrs Quincy were talking, and overhear bits like 'He's bought a private plot at the cemetery . . . she looked like an angel in her coffin . . . he's drinking like a fish . . . ' These confidences would end abruptly at my appearance.

One morning, just as I got back from Dr Scanlon's with my father's prescription, I walked into something that seemed like a nightmare. Mrs Quincy hadn't been in that morning, so it was probably a Saturday.

Strewn about the kitchen floor were the sheets that Nurse Parker used to use, and had left behind, as well as the nighties and pyjamas that had belonged to Mummy; on the table was the bottle of cologne that I had taken from the wardrobe.

'She would have wanted her little girl to have it, Terence!' Gran's voice was shrill.

'She's just a feckin' little thief. Nuttin', yer hear, nuttin' of hers is to be touched by any of yers.'

I stood in the doorway, terrified.

'Right, yer feckin' little scourge,' he said, looking up at me, 'so yer've bin in yer mother an' me's bedroom an' yer decided yer'd steal from yer own dead mother, God rest her, did yer?'

I didn't speak; I couldn't.

'Answer me, or I'll feckin' kill yers.'

'I didn't steal it, Mummy said I could have it.' I cried truthfully.

'She'd have told me if she'd have wanted t'give it ta the likes of yer,' he screamed, and wading through the heaped clothes on the floor, he hit me so violently that I fell.

'Don't you dare hit that child like that,' my grandmother yelled, picking me up and holding me to her.

'Don't tell me what I can or can't do wid my own feckin' daughter.'

'You're not doing to her what you did to my girl – everyone knows she married far beneath her. You're nothing but an Irish navvy, and my girl's lying in that cemetery because of you, you swine.'

'Get out, yer feckin' old biddy, yer've sponged off us long enough.'

'I've sponged off you? You didn't know what a fish knife was until you came into this family – thought it was for cutting cake, you ignorant swine. You swank about with my husband's cigarette case – you'd never seen gold before, had you?'

'Get out,' he screamed, 'get out, never set foot inside this house again! Irene told me about yer and yer wild parties and how yer spent every penny that was rightfully hers, and how many husbands have yer gone through who took what they wanted and pissed off, tell me that?'

'Irene wouldn't have said that, not my girl, you liar! Give me her father's cigarette case, she'd no right giving it to you!'

'I told yer, ole biddy, yer get nuttin'. She gave it to me so it wouldn't end up in "Uncle's" and never be redeemed.'

'If it belongs to anyone,' said Gran, 'it belongs to Alan. My God, why couldn't it have been you instead of him that was taken with *heart* trouble?'

'Get out, get out! I've never heard yer, yer wicked old bitch, talkin' about me to that other feckin' old biddy – she's out of a job yer can tell her that when yer seen her again! I'll phone up this afternoon an' tell them how she spent her time sittin' on her arse drinkin' tea wid yers.'

'And I'll phone your "fancy woman" at the Welfare and tell them about your drinking, and what you've just done to this child. I'll have them taken away from you,' proclaimed Gran.

He got up as if to strike her.

'Yes, you would hit an old woman and a child, you Irish scum, but you'll have hit out for the last time, because I'll kill you first, as surely as you killed my girl when you forced yourself on her and put her through another childbirth. You killed her! And I'm going to report you for what you did to that girl, make no mistake.' She stumbled out of the back door, high-pitched sobs coming from her throat.

'Pleased with yerself, are yer?' he said.

'No,' I whispered.

'Now, yer pick everythin' up off this floor an' yer fold it up, an' yer put it in the wardrobe in Mammy's and my room, and yer never – d'yer hear, never – go in there again.'

He was lifting my chin up so high that I thought my head would burst. Crying, I bent down and started picking up the sheets and other things. I folded them on the kitchen table, made two journeys to the front bedroom and laid the sheets and night-clothes on top of her shoes. Before locking the wardrobe, I placed the cologne back in the box, and wiped my face on her coat, feeling the familiar scent of her all around me.

Going back into the kitchen, I picked up his pills; they had fallen under Mummy's white rocking-chair, and now I put them on the table in front of him.

'Thank yer, darlin', he said, taking the wadding out of the top of the bottle, and throwing a handful of tablets down his throat.

He pulled me close to him. 'I'm sorry, darlin', does yer face hurt, let Daddy see? Hmm, it's a bit red, but it's no worse than one of yer brothers could have done.' He kissed my ear and cheek. 'Now listen, yer Granny was a foolish woman an' I think it's best we start again by just yer an' me an' the other four in this house, don't yer, sweetheart?'

'Yes.'

He'd never mentioned the episode following my mother's death until now, but he continued, 'When I took yer to see yers Mammy after she'd first died, Daddy didn't do it to frighten yer, it was just that she'd have wanted the two she loved best in the world wid her at that time – an' this is between the two of us, shall I tell yers what her last word was? Not me, oh no, it was "Caroline".'

I knew he was lying, she couldn't speak any more at the end; but this idea seemed to please him, so I went along with it, and suddenly I became afraid.

'Did she say anything else, Daddy?'

'Like what, darlin'?'

It came out in a rush then. There had been many things haunting me, things that at night would return as if to haunt my thoughts. The more I tried to switch them off, the more they loomed in front of me; the death scene he'd just recalled, the gaping hole in her back, the way he'd stood in the lavatory doorway as we tried to make our way into the front room, mocking us, but most of all the knock on the head that morning and her death that afternoon.

'Would a knock on the head have killed Mummy?' I asked.

'Oh God, no.' He was rocking me gently in his arms. 'That's a funny thing to be askin' yer Daddy, an' there must be a reason. Come on, my sweet, yers can tell yer ole Daddy anything. Just because Granny and I have had words, doesn't mean I'll not be going to see her an' bring her back, even though she said some wicked things to Daddy. Now c'mon.'

Out it all came, the reaching across for the feeder, the moans she'd made, my attempt to explain to Nurse Parker, that somehow didn't ever quite get explained after all.

'Darlin', darlin',' he said, 'we all knew, from the day the specialist came, that Mammy was goin' to be taken from us. Yer man told me, the reason Mammy had the dent in her head was because the growth was what's called "malignant", and would press against the bone and cause her terrible sufferin' – that's why they took that piece of bone away.' He was touching my head now, to illustrate what he meant. 'Now promise me, darlin', yer'll not be thinkin' these things any more?'

'I promise, Daddy. I'm sorry about the scent.'

'No, no, yer shall have it, now go and bring it back. Sure, yer Mammy would have wanted it for yers.'

He kissed me as I jumped down and once again took the cologne out of the box. Anna's crying outside brought me back with a bump; she'd cried for so long that her throat was rasping. I brought her in, saying I was sorry, and gave her pieces of melted chocolate that I'd bought for her earlier.

We didn't see Gran that Sunday. When my father came in Mrs Quincy had just washed the scullery floor and, true to his word, he said he'd like to talk to her. He sent us out in the rain while he did so. We didn't see Mrs Quincy again.

7

Miss Bowden called on the following afternoon, and the boys and I were sent into the front room to watch the test card on the television until Children's Hour came on. We had started back to school and had called at Gran's, arranging to meet her in Penn Gardens on Saturday mornings. She'd become a very old lady in just a few short weeks. We tried to keep up chatter that once would have brought an immediate response from her, but she no longer seemed to care. She kept up the ritual of buying us Smarties and pear drops, and giving us a 'spratt' each for pocket money.

One Saturday evening Timmy let the cat out of the bag about our clandestine meetings with Gran. 'I know who's behind this, yer feckin' little bitch,' he screamed at me. We were eating tea, and taking my plate from in front of me, he put it on the floor for Prowler, my cat, who couldn't believe his luck at the salmon and shrimp paste sandwiches set before him. Prowler looked up at him just once to check it was all OK, and quickly devoured the fish paste sandwiches.

Prowler had been a birthday present for me when I was six, and although most of his nights were spent on the tiles, he'd occasionally swagger in with a live mouse, with which he'd play football under the kitchen table, after severing the head – much to my horror and the boys' amusement. Rats he didn't bother to entertain us with, but would bring them in intact, as an offering. On the nights when he did come home, you'd find him sleeping next to me, paw around my neck. This summer had been one of plenty for Prowler; it was only rarely that I could manage to save enough out of my pocket money for a fivepenny tin of Kit-E-Kat, but this summer he'd eaten more Kit-E-Kat than he'd had in his whole life.

Carefully cutting the swiss roll into four thick chunks, my father put a huge piece in front of each of the boys and Anna, and told me I could drink my tea.

'Schemers like you don't get fed,' he said. 'An' by the way, it was a strange conversation I had with Dr Scanlon the other day about what a blow on der head can really do. He seems to think I was far too generous in my explanation to yers – I think yer'll know what it is I'm sayin', so before yer have any more thoughts about teachin' these little ones yer own sneaky ways, I'd think on my words.' My blood froze.

That night he went out, checking first on the food in the kitchen cabinet so that on his return he'd know if any had been taken. Tim got into trouble with the other boys, and started to cry. James collected up Tizer and lemonade bottles, and went and bought some crisps and chocolate.

Later I was awakened by a rough shaking and a torch being shone in my eyes.

'Away in the kitchen with yers, yer little bitch,' he said. Stumbling along with the cold linoleum under my feet, I walked into the kitchen. 'Would yers take a look at this?' he said. Half awake, I tried to make out the words on the white sheet of paper, and grasping the back of my neck, he pushed my head forward.

. . . and so, Mr O'Farrell, I read, it is with regret that I have to inform you that the cause of death was a blow to your wife's head . . . Yours faithfully, Dr Bassett, Pathologist.

Over and over he repeated those words, finally saying, 'but I'll be givin' yer one last chance,' and taking a match, he set light to the paper and threw it into the empty grate. This was to be the first of many nights when I would be shaken, and then the torch would be held in my eyes, so that most nights I would lie awake until sleep finally overcame me. Even now I still thank God I can remain in my bed, secure in the knowledge that I *can* remain there.

There was no one to tell, such was my guilt and shame, when, with winter come and the mornings freezing, I would be sent out to bring in coal and orange boxes, having to cross the dark yard, and always having trouble with the key that unlocked our coal shed. Sometimes he would creep out behind me as I was trying to find the coal in the dark, stepping over the two-foot-high wooden fence that kept the coal securely in on those rare days when Harvey the coal man had filled the cellar up.

'Murderer,' he would whisper as I struggled to chase and capture pieces of coal in the corner of the shed. I would scream and run, leaving the coal scuttle inside the shed, only to be frog-marched back out to collect it. The wood had to be cut with a hammer and knife, and I became adept at making a notch in the wood at the top, then grasping the knife handle at one side of the stake and bringing about the satisfying split of the wood with several hammer blows on the exposed side. If the strips of wood were long, I would make them as thin as possible, in order to break them easily. Some nights I would be allowed to sleep, though, and then I would awake with a start, expecting Anna to have been taken from my side.

Maggie, Mrs Williams, 'Auntie Ellen' and many more of my mother's friends tried several times to call, but I was sent to tell them that we were too busy to see anyone. Sometimes gifts were left and promptly thrown into the dustbin. We did not accept 'charity'. James was eventually dispatched with notes for the more persistent callers, asking them to refrain from calling while he, Terence, was trying to make a little family again, without too much intrusion from 'outside'.

The boys met their friends in the air-raid shelter that was our 'den'. I asked them if anyone had enquired what was going on, but the boys didn't seem able to enlighten me, except to tell me that most of the lads were scared of the 'old man'. My friend Gina no longer bothered to call for me, she had become used to my being unable to go out to play because I had to look after the baby. I watched, bitterly hurt, from the front room window as she walked past with her arms round a girl called Shirley.

One night we were watching the TV when he came home, unexpectedly early, but expectedly drunk. The boys were making a 'guy' for the November 5th celebrations – the boys were late that year because some of the lads had already booked their pitches for 'penny for the guy'. The room was strewn with bits of paper and string, and an old pair of his pin-striped trousers were lying prone on the floor, stuffed with paper.

'Jesus Christ, what d'yer think yer doin' here?' He tottered over to the TV, switching it off, then, picking up the trousers, he threw the paper round the floor. Anna started to cry, and so did Tim. James sat on the floor, head bent, clenching and unclenching his fists, while Patrick was deathly white, looking at me as if I could remedy the situation, or, perhaps believing that it was all going to be some poor joke at their expense.

'Now, yer little bastards, yers can clean up every bit of this mess. I want to walk into this room and find everything shipshape d'yer hear?'

'Yes,' I answered, taking the initiative.

'I didn't hear the rest of yers!'

'Yes,' said the other three, trying to pick up the paper. James put the first ball on the fire.

'So yer goin' to set the feckin' house alight, are yers,' Dad screamed.

The boys made several trips out to the dustbins and back again. When we had tidied the room, and brought his trousers through and folded them over the back of the winged rocking-chair, he said I was to put the iron on and press back the creases.

James took Anna from me without any questioning, and they sat drinking the cocoa I had made them with water and just a dash of milk and saccharins. I'd buttered some cream crackers, the only things to eat left in the kitchen cabinet. Anna was playing around with her bottle of cocoa, while I finished putting the crease in the old trousers. I gave them to him to inspect, and he didn't seem to know what I'd been doing.

'Murderer!' he whispered. I felt my bowels constrict. Had the boys heard? 'I've somethin' to tell yers all, an' yer gonna listen, sure yer are.' No God, please no, don't tell the boys. They'd each spent many nights crying for Mummy, and then for Gran; sometimes one (usually James) would start the others off, and they'd cry out for both of them. What would they do to me if they knew I was the one who was responsible? They were, after all, the only thing I had now that we shared a common bond of grief. Anna had begun to call me 'Mummy Caroo', and did so now, putting her arms out for me to take her, which I did.

'Yers all done a very silly thing an' I think yers know that means I have t'punish yers, so from now on the front room is locked to yers. I've a key, so yers tryin' anything clever will do yers no good. Now, yer've the kitchen, the scullery and yer bedroom, don't be lookin' sorry for yerselves; sure, there are people in the old country eatin', cookin', an' sleepin' in one room, ten at a time – so yers are very lucky. Now, get out, an' say "Goodnight, God bless" to yer Daddy.'

We each bent to kiss him, and as I held Anna down to kiss him, and put my lips against his cheek, he whispered, 'Thought I'd be blowin' the whistle on yers, then, did yers?' I didn't quite know what 'blowing the whistle' meant, but I guessed he was just telling me he had let me off – this time.

That night, as the boys and I lay in bed, the two younger ones crying for the loss of their 'guy' and the TV, James reassured them about the guy (though there was little he could do about the TV). 'Look, we'll call a meeting with the lads in the den, they'll help us with a new guy.'

'Are you going to tell them what's happened to the guy?' I asked.

'Yes, I fucking am,' said James.

'Sshh . . . James, don't swear. If he hears you!'

'Listen,' James whispered quietly, 'do you know where he keeps his pills?'

'Yes, he keeps some in the drawer in the front room and some on top of the kitchen cabinet. Why?'

'I'll tell you tomorrow,' promised James.

During this time my father wasn't getting pills from Dr Scanlon alone. I would often have to take the morning off school to go on the bus to a doctor's surgery in Muswell Hill, and sometimes to yet another, an Asian doctor in Finsbury Park. I never did quite know how he'd acquired all these doctors, but I knew that sometimes when I came back he'd be very pleased with me, and he could stay that way for the rest of that day and night.

The day following the 'guy' incident was such a time, and my father made me take the whole day off school; I went to collect Anna early that afternoon. The boys' tea was prepared before I left for the nursery and they were able to go off early for their meeting in the den, too. James told me that night that all the boys had been 'great' and were going to contribute some of their takings; on the following Saturday morning they were going up to Pete Williams's to make another guy – Mrs Williams would find some suitable clothes. As Dad had been in such a good mood earlier that evening, the boys had hoped that he would forget his threat of the night before; when he went out, he bent and kissed us all, leaving half a crown for some Tizer or sweets. When the boys tried the front-room door, though, it was locked.

Life at home was leaving me exhausted, with the housework to cope with, the never-ending problem of drying clothes around the fire-guard, going to the bag-wash and bringing it home, sometimes having to sit Anna on top of the damp, heavy sack. My school work was suffering. One morning, during a double domestic science lesson, a teacher new to the school was going to teach us to make cheese scones. Suddenly, as she saw me weighing the flour, she pounced.

'Caroline O'Farrell! Come here! Girls! Girls! I want you all to come over here, and at once! Now, Caroline, I believe you have something to show us, haven't you?'

'No, Madam,' I answered, perplexed.

'But, my dear, you have. Now girls, open your hands, palms first. No, not yours, Caroline. Now the backs. Good! Gillian Brown, stand over there next to Caroline. Now, Gillian, first of all let us see your palms – good. And over.'

I knew, as I looked at the assorted hands, some sporting bitten finger-nails, what it was about, and my legs were trembling. Gill's finger-nails were chewed right down, and they were ink-stained and grubby. Mine were broken and a bluey-blackness was indelibly etched into the nail-bed surrounds – this was the general hue of the skin all over my hands. On the backs there were thin spider-web breaks in the skin, and blood had dried in minute patches on the chapped skin.

'You two girls will not enter these kitchens again until your hands are suitable to touch my stove and utensils. Now, get out, scrub your hands, come back to me after you have done so.'

Gillian muttered 'old cow' when we were outside the door, and we made our way to the cloakrooms. The regulation school soap took most of the ink away, and the grubbiness went from Gill's hands, but mine only came up a little bit cleaner, and the skin broke and caused more threads of fresh blood to appear. I could do nothing much more with my nails. We went back into the classroom and Gillian was allowed to resume cooking, but I was sent back to the empty classroom to write 'I must remember hygiene in the kitchen at all times' one hundred times.

I had been hurt and humiliated in front of the whole class, and I remembered then clearing out the ashes from the fire in the mornings or taking the old leather bag up to Harvey's coal yard for fourteen pounds of slack. I tried to think what I could do to get my nails clean. I don't know how I got through the rest of the day, but that night, when I arrived back with Anna, Dad asked me where the scones were.

'Yer sure yer didn't burn 'em now?' I burst into tears. He put his arms around me and I told him what had happened. He sent James out for a nail brush, and, after cutting my nails, he scrubbed at them with Vim until they were quite clean, then he applied Vaseline to the backs and the nails which were raw. That night Dad washed up, having bound up my hands with some of the sheeting from the cupboard, which had acquired the name of the 'nosebleed sheet', as I had had several nosebleeds.

My father told me to stay away from school in the morning, as he'd be going to see not only the offending teacher, but the headmistress too. That morning I prayed, after I got back from taking Anna to nursery. Oh how I prayed! What would he say to them? What would they say to me? Would I be expelled? He came back at about eleven o'clock, smiling. 'Well, I think you'll find an apology from that jumped up bitch of a teacher. That headmistress of yours – Doctor whatever – wonderful woman, sure she made that little galley maid look two inches high, sure she did. Yer go in this afternoon and they'll be all over yer. Did yer know yer Doctor sent her away to get us a tray of tea and biscuits?'

Sure enough, that afternoon both Dr Barton and the domestic science teacher were in the Head's office when I was summoned. The teacher explained that she was unaware of my home background, and if there was anything she could do ... terribly sorry, misconstruing slovenliness with unexplained sad home circumstances ... I felt sorry for her as I left the office. All the girls were waiting to hear what had happened, and I was a heroine for the next two days. After all, everyone always said their Mam or Dad would be 'up the school', but it was a rare thing for the threat to be carried out. Such was my father's perversity that he would allow no outsider to humiliate his children, and it didn't need too much imagination to work out how he'd played on the sympathy of the teachers and had them feeling guilty.

On bonfire night I stood at the end of the street with Anna in my arms, wrapped up in a blanket. Anna liked the Roman candles, the Catherine wheels and the fire itself, but the bangers and jumping jacks had frightened her, so I had to take her in. The two windows from which we could have watched were both in the front, looking out onto the street – but we were not allowed to enter either room. I made Anna a bottle and gave her some chocolate out of the money the boys had made 'guying'; they'd managed to give me a shilling. I lay down in the darkness with Anna, and remembered all the other bonfire nights, and cried.

8

The following night I walked home through the streets, smelling the air still rank with gunpowder, and saw the ashes of the bonfires. At home it smelt good in the kitchen. Dad had made jacket potatoes for us, and as usual the boys had that air of expectancy about them which meant 'Maybe he'll relent and let us watch TV tonight'. But he went out and the room remained locked. Now that the season of Guy Fawkes was over, the outlook was bleak indeed as we sat in the kitchen playing 'Hangman' or 'Boxes'.

That night I was awakened again by the torch beam shining in my eyes.

'Get out, get out,' he said. The familiar terror was back with me as he pushed me along the cold passage-way. 'OK, yer little bastard, where are they?'

'What?' I asked, beginning to cry.

'Me feckin' tablets, that's what.'

'I don't know. I gave them to you before we went out to look at the fire – Mr Ward will tell you, I did get them.'

'I know yers feckin' got them, but I want to know where yer've put 'em, or maybe yers just want me t'die the same way as yer killed yer poor sainted Mammy?'

'No!' I cried, 'I wouldn't do that.'

'Yers think I can keep quiet about the letter from the hospital givin' me feckin' news that yer killed yer own sainted mother. Well, yer lyin' little banshee, I'm not so stupid as to throw away a letter like that, sure I wouldn't, I've a copy, an' if yer don't hand over the feckin' tablets, it'll be the police station for yers tonight.'

'No, please no, I haven't had them!'

He pulled my hair back and began hitting my face; blood started to run from my nose. Then he let me go; blood was seeping through the hand I had cupped over my nose, falling in regular splashes on the floor.

'Clean that shit up!' he screamed. He was shaking violently. 'Yer'll clean these decks until they sparkle!' He stood there watching as I went to the cupboard to fetch my 'nosebleed sheet'. I tore it in strips, then went into the scullery and held a piece of cloth under the tap. I held my head back, feeling the blood in my throat, then I bent over to start wiping up the blood spots, but they only multiplied as I bent to wash them away.

'Sit in that chair 'til that mess stops,' he said, 'an' think about whether or not yer goin' to give me the pills.'

'I haven't . . . '

'Yer gonna pay dearly for this stroke.'

He left the room, and I could hear him turning out drawers. When the bleeding had stopped, I got up and very gingerly began to wash my feet and legs, hands and wrists, then my face and neck. Then I started to clean up the blood from the floor, after which I put the kettle on, and began washing up the cups and putting them on the kitchen table.

Suddenly, as I tried to wash the sugar from the bottom of Dad's cup, my heart stood still. The morning after we had been banished from the front room, James had got up early and had discussed, quite seriously, whether or not we would grind the tablets down and put all of them in his tea. I had told him they tasted bitter, and we'd never get away with it, but just supposing. Oh God, Jimmy, no you wouldn't!

I didn't hear my father come back in, and I jumped.

'Get those pills for me, yer little bastard,' he whispered. 'Yer a murderer, d'yer hear? an' the world's gonna know by tomorrow just what yer did to yer Mammy unless I get the pills.' I began looking frantically for the pills. 'Now yer've made a big play-act about lookin' for 'em, yer can light the feckin' fire.'

I went into the yard, taking the coal-shed key, and brought back some pieces of orange box. He watched as I took the knife and hammer from under the sink and, pulling back the fire-guard, began to sift the bigger cinders from the ash, putting them to one side. I took the knife and started to split through the wood, leaving the ashes in the tray to cool before throwing them away.

'Faster, yer lazy little bitch,' he chided. 'Look what it is yer have in yer hands — now what are they? I didn't hear yers, what are they?'

'Wood,' I said.

'Yes, an' what else?'

'A hammer and knife.' I stammered.

'And d'yer know what a hammer and knife is?'

'Yes, they — '

'No, I best tell yers, they're both instruments that are used by murderers t'kill, an' bein' one yerself, yer should be faster wid yer deadly weapons!'

Tears spilled on my knees, like a weak blood solution – I'd hit a notch in the wood, and it wouldn't budge. I twisted and pulled, tying to get the knife out, and in a flash he was on me. I heard the crack of the wood as he freed the knife, then, pulling me up, he thrashed at my fingers with the knife. The pain took a while to reach the point where the knife had sliced across the tops of the fingers of my left hand.

He watched as the blood began to pour down my hand and wrist and on to the floor, then took the 'nosebleed sheet' and tore furiously at the material, binding strips round and round my hand. He reached to the top of the kitchen cabinet.

'Germolene . . . where the feckin . . . ' He picked up the tin of ointment – and something else: the bottle of pills. He took four, and then another, then brought me the cup he had just drunk from, and tore an Aspro from a pink strip.

'Oh God, darlin',' he said, unbinding the blood-soaked rag. 'Oh forgive me, darlin' forgive me.'

I was in such pain. He was on his knees now, holding my thin, cold legs to him. 'Please say yer'll forgive me, darlin'?'

'Yes, Daddy.' He gently put Germolene over the fingers, but the bleeding did not stop, and the middle finger gaped open like a small mouth. He bound them tightly. Next he relit the kettle and made tea for us both. I was sitting in Mummy's rocking-chair, drinking tea, and he told me I mustn't go to school in the morning; instead I must go to Ward the chemist and get the fingers dressed properly.

He started the fire and went to collect some more coal, then washed the more recent blood-stains from the hearth and the floor before ushering me back to bed. I went to sleep with Anna, but my fingers were throbbing and I was very cold.

After I took Anna to nursery that morning, I was given a pound note, plus a shopping list that Dad had left on the table. Mr Ward at the chemist was old, with white hair, and very kind. He asked me how the accident happened. I longed to tell him the truth, but I myself was a murderer, and even kind old Mr Ward would show me no compassion if he knew, so I told him I had taken a knife from the drawer the 'wrong way'. I went into the back of the pharmacy, and he took me to the window at the back to examine my hand. He told me that the middle finger needed stitching.

'Oh no,' I said, 'I can't do that.'

He turned my face to one side, and seemed to be looking under my hair.

'Ummm . . . well, let's see what I can do for these fingers.'

I winced as he began to tape up the middle one, trying to close the wound with elastoplast; he gave less attention to the others, then made an overall bandage.

'Was anyone with you when this happened?' he asked.

'No, Mr Ward.'

He stood there looking at me for a long time, while I held out the pound note.

'No, no, no, m'dear,' he said. 'What I would like you to do for me is to go and see Dr Scanlon and have some stitches put in.'

'Yes, I will, Mr Ward. Thank you very much.'

I ran out of the chemist's and along to Mr Forrester for some Players and the *Daily Mail*, two ounces of blue cheese from the Co-op, and a loaf, then my shopping was done.

'Perhaps he'll be in a good mood,' I thought, 'and then I'll ask him if I can go to the library for him. He's got his tablets, paper, blue cheese – a book usually cheers him up.'

I went in through the back door and put the things away. Then I set out the paper and his cigarettes on a tray, put the kettle on, and made up the fire while I waited for the kettle to boil, careful not to get my bandage dirty.

There was music playing somewhere in the building. I thought I'd heard it earlier as I came down the passage-way with Anna, but what with the boys and the general rush in the kitchen this morning, I had forgotten about it. Now I went out into the passage. The sound was more like a knock, knock – a tiny knocking. Maybe Prowler was locked in our bedroom? As I passed the front room I could hear that it seemed to be coming from there, but I went to our bedroom anyway. My hand was still throbbing.

The sound was definitely coming from the front room. I went into the kitchen, made a pot of tea, and put Dad's cup on the tray. I learned never to call his name, but to knock on the door and wait to be granted admission – but this time I got no response from either door, so I went back to the kitchen with the tray. Then I knocked again on the front-room door. There was a definite noise from within, so, trembling, I opened the door. The first thing my eyes alighted on was the Dansette record player, which had stuck. Frank Sinatra was singing 'Oh how . . . oh how . . . oh how . . . ' to 'These Foolish Things'.

My eyes wandered across to where my father's inert figure was sprawled, one leg and an arm on the floor. His face was as contorted as his body.

'No!' I screamed, 'No, God, Mummy, please help me!'

I saw a note lying next to the empty bottle of morphine tablets. I took it and ran from the room in terror, away, away from death as I had done only four months ago. I read the note, and the horror and shock were worse than his death: *Dear little murderer, I have gone to join your Mammy so that together we can bring about an end to my suffering and ask the Holy Mother to forgive you for . . .*

I screamed and screamed. Taking the paper and screwing it into a ball, I threw it on to the fire, crushing the blackened paper to ash. Somehow I dragged myself back into that room of death to see if there was any more of the letter. Perhaps he'd used two sheets? It was then that I noticed he was breathing, his nostrils drawing in and out like the gills of a fish.

I ran from the house, along the main road, to the public telephone box outside the library. To think that two years ago we had desperately wanted to phone someone up! But apart from Auntie Ruth (who would not have been pleased) there was no one – and the one thing we'd always wanted to do, but never dared, was to dial 999.

'Which service do you require?' The operator answered straight away.

'Ambulance, please come quickly, he's dying.' I gave the address and hung up.

I hadn't reached the Mansions when I heard the clanging of ambulance bells. I ran back inside to wait, and to make sure that there was no trace of the note left in the ashes. No one must ever know. 'He did it for me too, didn't he?' I thought. When I opened the door there was a stretcher there, with red blankets.

'Where's your mummy, darling?' the ambulance driver asked.

'She's dead, but my daddy's in there, I think he's dead too.'

'Stay out there, love,' called one of the ambulance men.

'Better get a move on, Bert.'

I pressed my cheek against the cool wall. It felt bruised.

'We might have a DOA.' I heard another voice say.

'Are you on your own, sweetheart?' called the man who'd done all the talking.

'Yes, my brothers are in school, and my baby sister's in nursery.' I was trying not to cry.

'Well, what are we going to do with you, eh?'

They were manipulating the stretcher through the door now, but I couldn't see if they'd covered his head up or not. If they had, it meant he was dead, I'd seen that on the pictures; but I couldn't make out anything except a glimpse of the red blanket.

'Now, you promise to stay here, darling, and we'll get someone along to see you right away. So promise you'll stay put, eh?'

'Yes,' I said, closing the door and catching sight of the crowd that had assembled at the entrance of the Mansions.

'Out the bloody way, will you?' I heard, as I closed the door. Maybe Maggie would come, but I'd promised to stay, so I couldn't go over to her. The front-room door was wide open, and I saw the ambulance race past the window, there, its bell clanging urgently. I looked into the room. The only evidence that this had not been a nightmare was two damp patches on the settee. I looked on the floor for the tablet bottle, but it had gone.

I closed the door, but not before I'd picked up the record arm to put it in its place – I got a small electric shock. This seemed to be the final, ultimate hurt, and as I held the hand that had received the shock in my bandaged one, I too wanted to die, for the first time in my life, and the thought that I could do so by my own hand filled me with fear and awe.

I began to run wildly through the house. I'd hidden the pink chiffon scarf in a mouse hole in the kitchen cupboard, and I pulled it out with difficulty. It was shredded, but as I held it to my nose, the faint scent of 'Evening in Paris' that was my mother came through the musty smell. I wound the soft pink cloth around my hand, and ran it over my eyes, nose and mouth. 'Come back, Mummy,' I called to the empty walls, but no one answered.

I lay on the bed I shared with Timmy and Anna, my breath coming in shudders. Someone was knocking on the front door, and at the same time I saw my father's tall figure pass the back bedroom window through the lace curtain. He'd played a trick on me! How had he got away from the ambulance men – or had there been any such incident? Was I going mad? Footsteps were coming up the passage-way. It was *his* walk. Quickly I rolled under the bed, pulling the blue blanket down to the floor to hide myself. Supposing he was dead, and had come back to haunt me? Wasn't he always saying that he would give three knocks and return?

The front door was being opened, and I could hear men's voices as it was closed again. A great shudder and sigh shook my thin body, and I inhaled fluff, grey and soft, from under the bed; it was slimy in my mouth, and made me want to sneeze as I tried to remove it with my unbandaged hand. They were knocking, and trying the door to the front bedroom, and eventually I heard heavy footsteps enter our room. I held my breath. I could see a glimpse of black shoes – they were big, very big, like his. I held my breath and shut my eyes tight.

'Here, Bob, in here, mate.' It wasn't him; there was no accent.

I kept my eyes closed, but I felt a large hand gently pulling me from under the bed.

'Come on, sweetheart.' His voice was gentle – but *his* voice was gentle too. No one could say 'murderer' more gently than him!

Deftly those big hands slid me a little way further across the linoleum and up into the air. I kept my eyes tightly shut all the time.

'See if you can make a brew, Bob.'

The soft voice was near to my face now. I opened my eyes for the first time, and saw a bluish chin, with a strap captured in one of the many folds. I closed my eyes again – oh, why couldn't I faint like they did in the films.

'There, there, sweetheart,' he was saying; we were moving down the hallway now, towards the kitchen. I opened my eyes as we approached the kitchen, and the first thing I saw was a policeman's helmet on the open flap of the kitchen cabinet. A familiar throbbing began in my spine. A young policeman with short blond hair was bringing a cup of tea to me, in the toothbrush beaker.

'Here now, darling,' said 'Chins', as he sat me down in the rocking-chair, and, bending down, put the beaker to my lips. It tasted of Gibbs toothpaste, but I drank the tea as he told me. 'Now, darling don't be frightened,' said 'Chins', 'Just call me Uncle Jim OK? You've had a shock, but I want you to tell Uncle Jim everything – take your time.'

I said nothing. They knew, I was sure they knew; if Dad had made a copy of the report on why Mummy had died, I was sure they must have found a copy of his note. I wondered vaguely if there was a Black Maria outside, waiting to take me away. I knew they couldn't hang me, like they had Ruth Ellis – it didn't seem long ago that Mummy was collecting names on a list so that she wouldn't hang. Still, I supposed there was something like a prison for girls, just as there were Borstals for boys. But who would take care of the boys and Anna? I began to cry.

'I hurt my hand on a knife,' I said.

'Is that why you aren't in school, love?'

'Yes.'

'And I understand your Mummy's ... er ... dead?'

'Yes.'

'How long ago, sweetheart?'

'Oh ages, back in the summer.'

I went on to tell him about the boys and Anna. Then he asked me who looked after us, and I said Daddy did.

'Haven't you got no aunties or uncles, love?'

'Yes, I've got an Auntie Ruth, but we don't see her now Uncle Alan's ill. But we've got a Granny.'

'Where's she then, darling?'

I gave him Gran's address, but told him if she wasn't there she'd be at Auntie Ruth's. I didn't know where my auntie lived, but she was on the telephone – though I drew a blank when he asked me for her surname.

'Does Granny come to see you?'

'No, not since Mummy died' – careful, I thought, don't say anything else.

'What schools do you all go to?' I told him. 'Oh, so you're a Grammar girl, eh? Now, did anything unusual happen last night or this morning?' he asked, looking at my hand.

'Only I cut my hand on a knife in the drawer, and Mr Ward put a bandage on it. He's the chemist.'

'Oh yes, I know Mr Ward,' he said. 'Nice man, that. He won't bless you when he sees the colour of that bandage.'

It was already grey and dirty from my stay under the bed.

'Was your Dad OK when you went to school this morning?'

'Oh, he didn't get up, but he's had his lung out, and he sometimes doesn't.'

'And you get those brothers and that little sister off to school then, do you?'

'Yes, but we manage all right.'

'I think I'll borrow you, and take you home with me to teach my kids a thing or two! – So, getting back to this morning, can you tell me what happened?'

I told him everything that had happened, with the exception of the note. When I looked towards the fire, it was dying.

'Now look, there's a lady coming in a minute, and she's going to take you away for a few days.'

What did he mean – take me away? 'What about Anna and the boys?' I started to cry.

'What makes you think they won't be taking them along with you, eh?'

'But they haven't done anything!' I yelled, jumping off the chair and making for the door into the passage-way. The policeman without a helmet was blocking my escape through the scullery door.

'Jim' lumbered up the hallway after me, and I ran straight into Miss Bowden, the pretty lady who'd been to see Dad before.

'Hey there, Caroline,' she said, catching hold of my coat.

'You took your time,' said Jim, from behind me.

'I came as soon as I could.' She spoke abruptly. 'Now, listen, you go with Uncle Bob and get some fish and chips for your dinner. You must be starving.'

I wasn't, but the young policeman, who was now wearing his helmet, took me over the road to the chip shop. People were looking at us strangely as the policeman went with me into 'Joe's'.

'Do you want fish, love?' asked the young policeman.

'No thank you, just chips,' I said. I wanted to say 'just nothing', but perhaps they'd think I was being awkward.

'Make that skate and chips twice as well,' said the young policeman to Joe. Joe was looking nonplussed. 'What you been up to, Curly?' he asked. I saw the policeman frown at Joe.

'She's a good kid, that'n,' said Joe quickly, sensing that he'd put his foot in it. 'They're on the house,' he added.

'Thanks guv',' said the policeman.

We made our way back across the road, the policeman holding my hand. Curious looks came from the passers-by. The big policeman – Uncle Jim – and

Miss Bowden were standing in the kitchen when we got back.

'Well, young lady, we've got to go now, but Miss Bowden will take good care of you, and I promise that I'll come and see you when you get back from your little holiday — Oh good,' Uncle Jim added, seeing the wrapped newspaper in the young policeman's hand. 'You're learning fast, Bob. Skate, is it?'

'Yes,' replied Bob. 'On the house, too!'

'Good, good,' said Uncle Jim. He bent down and gave me a kiss. 'Got to go and have our dinner now, darling. You'll be keeping in touch?' he said to Miss Bowden.

'Yes,' she replied.

'Bye then, darling,' and they had both gone.

'Would you like some chips?' I asked Miss Bowden.

'No, thank you, Caroline, but I'd love a cup of tea.'

I told her about the policeman making a cup in the tooth mug, and we both laughed.

9

After we'd finished our tea, Miss Bowden said, 'You've had some pretty nasty things happen today, Caroline, and now we've got to make some nice things happen. First of all, as I can call you Caroline, I think you should call me Joan. OK?'

'Yes, OK,' I replied. She really was pretty; her fair hair was drawn back from her face, and her curls were prettily arranged on top. She wore a camel coat and a full, brown wool skirt with brown peep-toe high-heeled shoes. She reminded me of someone, but I couldn't remember who, though her hairstyle reminded me a bit of the one Mummy had before they shaved off her curls, leaving her head looking as blue as Uncle Jim the policeman's chin.

She helped me wash up the few dishes, and suddenly Prowler was scratching at the back door. I let him in.

'Is this your cat?' Joan asked.

'Yes,' I said, picking him up and letting him lick my face. I poured him some milk into a saucer. 'No Kit-E-Kat today, Prowler,' I told him.

'Haven't you any food in the house for him?'

'No, he only has his Kit-E-Kat when we can afford it, but he does all right at the fishmonger's and other places,' I said.

'Well, he doesn't look as if he's starving to death,' she laughed, stroking him. Ignoring her, he carried on lapping his milk.

'Now, do you have any suitcases?' asked Joan.

'There's a big one under James and Patrick's bed, but it belongs to Daddy, and he may not allow us . . .'

'Come on, I'll go and get it, and you get as many things as you can together – what you think you'll need for a week or so.'

That wasn't difficult. The summer feast had produced a winter famine, and we had very little in the way of winter clothes. I began to gather Anna's abrasively hard nappies from the fire-guard, along with some of the boys' socks and pants, and some damp woollen leggings and coatees of Anna's. The bedroom drawers yielded only a few jumpers and odd pyjama tops and bottoms. We put some wellingtons into a big bag, and I found two clean 'scratchy' towels.

As we tried to shut the big suitcase, I saw that one of the boys' grey socks had fallen to the hearth, and looking into the sleepy fire, I thought I saw some more of the letter. I quickly retrieved the sock and was bending over the fire-guard when Joan came back into the room carrying some of the boys' books and an old grey woollen lamb of Anna's.

'What are you doing, dear?' asked Joan, as she saw me stabbing at the fire.

'I was just going to make up the fire,' I lied. 'Let it die down,' she said. 'We've got a very busy afternoon ahead of us, you and I.'

Several times Joan asked me if I wanted to talk about home, and I was more than willing to discuss the boys and Anna, but she knew as well as I did that I was being evasive when asked about Dad.

'Why is the other bedroom locked?' she'd asked.

'Because all the pills are kept in there,' I answered swiftly.

62

'Very wise,' she commented.

'Where are we going?' I asked.

'To my office,' was all she would say.

It wasn't very far to her office, and I wondered why I had never noticed it before. She sat me in a little waiting room with a *Woman* magazine, and someone brought me a doughnut and a cup of tea. Eventually Joan reappeared. 'Sorry to have been so long, love,' she said.

I hadn't minded. It was warm in the little waiting room, and the magazine had been full of things about Christmas, but now she told me we were just going shopping, and my thoughts immediately sprang to Anna and the boys. I'd lost track of time. I didn't want to appear rude, and I wouldn't have minded going to get her shopping for her myself, and said so, as long as I wouldn't be late to collect Anna. The back door was locked too, so that boys couldn't get in.

Joan laughed, then looking down at my ankle socks, the tops of which were patterned with rivulets of blood from my chapped legs, she frowned, and took me back down the stairs. We caught a bus to the department store where Granny and I had shopped for my mother, and she took me to the children's department, and there bought two pairs of long fawn woollen socks, two vests, two pairs of pants (one navy blue for school and one white), a green V-necked jumper and a school blouse, and a pair of green woollen gloves. Down in the shoe department, she bought a pair of wellingtons and some brown school lace-up shoes. She seemed to be able to pay for all this just by signing a white slip of paper.

When she took me into Lyons Corner House for a cup of tea and a cheesecake, my anxiety about the boys and Anna could no longer be contained. I was, among other things, suspicious of why she was doing all this, but I tried to explain to her that the boys had only two pairs of socks each, and it wasn't just me who had cut-up Shredded Wheat card in my shoes. They only had one pair of trousers each, I told her, and I listed all their poor wardrobe, finishing with the fact that Anna's buckskin boots were the only ones she had, and she'd thrown one down the toilet. When I dried it in front of the fire, it had come up all stiff and she limped. Joan didn't seem to understand their plight, and I felt angry, but I rested my case and pleaded with her that it was time to collect Anna and the boys.

As we took the bus back to her office, it was dark, and I began to think that perhaps they were going to send me away, away from my family. She held my hand as we climbed the stairs. Perhaps he had died, and had named me as a murderer in a final confession on his deathbed. What was it the policeman Jim had said — 'We'll keep in touch' or something like that. She kept trying to soothe me, but all I knew was that it was cold and dark out there, and Anna and the boys would be waiting. Someone would have Anna at the nursery, but the boys — perhaps they'd have the sense to go to the Williamses.

There were other kids making a lot of noise now in the room I had been in before; I could hear a baby shrieking. It was all too much. I went into Joan's office with her, and we both put our packages on her desk.

'Come on,' she said, leading me back to the room those kids were hollering in; as I walked through the door, it was with total disbelief that I saw James and Patrick arguing over some comics. Timmy was pulling a duck on a string while Anna waddled after it as fast as she could to catch its wings, which were flapping as Timmy pulled it along — this sent her into even more shrieks of laughter. I ran to them, kissing them all over and over again.

One corner of the small room was stacked with bags of all shapes and sizes, and shoe and boot boxes sat alongside them. The boys all tried to tell me at once what clothing they'd been bought, as well as comics, and food in a café. A Mrs Pearce had been responsible for *their* shopping, along with a Miss Green. Anna just wanted to show off her duck the whole time, while the boys told me about their new wellies and gloves and trousers with a back pocket. It was 'Mrs Pearce did this', and 'Mrs Pearce did that', until at last Mrs Pearce herself walked in.

'This is the little mother Caroline, is it?' She came over and gently held my hand. 'Well, Miss Bowden and I won't be a minute. She has to make some telephone calls, and I've made you all a warm drink and some biscuits. Won't be a tick.'

'Jimmy, did they tell you what happened?' I asked.

'Yes. Daddy was in such great pain,' James threw his hand dramatically across his chest, 'that he accidentally took too many tablets, poor man! But he'll live — worse luck! What happened to your hand?'

'What did he do?' asked Patrick, joining us. 'Tell us. We won't tell, honest.'

'I'll tell you later,' I said, as I saw the door opening and jumped up to give

Mrs Pearce a hand with the tray of tea and biscuits. Anna, tired now of her game with the duck, came over and stretched out her arms to me. 'Bot-bot, Mummy Caroo,' she said, over and over. I saw that the suitcase and bag had also been brought from home, but I realized that I hadn't packed her bottle. I explained this to Mrs Pearce, who said she'd see what she could do, and came back about ten minutes later with a new Maws feeding bottle and two different-sized teats. Anna complained about the unfamiliarity of the new teat, but eventually settled back in my arms with a bottle of hot milk, water and sugar, and fell fast asleep, her little hand, as always, twining its fingers round my hair.

The boys were beginning to get restless, and James and Patrick were dying to know what had happened to my hand. Timmy, who was sitting on the other side of me, on a hard wooden chair, sucking his thumb, suddenly started crying. 'I wanna go home,' he wailed. Just then Joan appeared; I'd begun to think that maybe she'd gone home.

'Right,' she said. 'How would you all fancy going for a holiday in the country for a week or so?'

'Do you mean all of us together?' I asked.

'Yes.'

'Is it a farm?' asked Patrick.

'No, it's not a farm, Patrick, but it has farms around it,' replied Mrs Pearce.

'No. It's in what is called a new Garden City,' said Joan, 'and there's a lovely family, Mr and Mrs Coleman, who have one little girl, Marie, and they want you to come and stay very much.'

'When will we be going?' I asked.

'They're expecting us all in about two hours,' said Joan.

'It can't be in the country then,' said James. 'It takes more than two hours to get to the country from here.' I kicked him with my foot.

'Wha's that for?' asked James indignantly.

'Why can't Gran come and take us home?' asked Timmy sleepily.

'Because, darling,' said Joan, 'Gran's an old lady, and she's not very well at the moment, but as soon as she's better . . . '

At that point a young man came in; he said his name was Dennis Simpson. He was holding five 'lucky bags' in his hand. He dropped the bags on the floor. Timmy was suddenly wide awake, scrambling with the other two on the floor; as they felt the contents, they began to swap the bags.

'These are for girls,' said Timmy, bringing two pink bags over to me.

'What do you say to Mr Simpson, boys?' I asked.

'Thank you very much,' they chanted.

'Thank you, Mr Simpson,' I said, putting the two pink lucky bags on the seat beside me. I asked if we were going on the tube or the bus.

'In a car.'

'A car?' the three boys echoed.

'Yep — and I'd like it better if you all call me Dennis.'

'OK Dennis,' said James.

'We'd better make a move then,' he said, 'Give us a hand, lads.'

The bags were distributed amongst the boys, and Dennis took the suitcase and some of the shoe boxes, though finally the boxes had to be abandoned as too cumbersome, and the new boots and shoes were carefully put under our feet in the back seat.

The boys all wanted the impossibility of a seat by the window. Anna woke up and started to whimper, and her whimpering grew to a loud cry as we set off, sitting on the cold leather seats of the black Hillman and waving our goodbyes to Mrs Pearce. I couldn't find her bottle on the car seat anywhere, but when Joan offered to take her into the front, her screams in the confines of the car were so great that once again I received her back into my aching arms. My hand was throbbing quite badly now. Eventually James found the bottle stuck in a wellington on the floor. I quickly put the bottle back in her mouth and she went back to sleep. The hum of the engine and the rocking movement made me feel sleepy too.

It was our first ride in a private car, and James said, 'I hope Pete Matthews sees us, and Paul, yeah, an' Ronnie Nelson an' . . . ' On and on they went.

'Hey, Mr Dennis,' said James, as if the thought had only just struck him, 'Can we drive round home just quickly to see if any of our mates can see us?'

'I don't see why not,' said Dennis, laughing. He drove around the block slowly, just as those other cars had, back in the summer. The only person about was Derek Matthews, who was finishing his paper round, and didn't recognize the occupants of the black car who were hammering against the car window. The boys were settling down now, as we left the yellow, damp-laden air of the London streets behind. There was an aura of expectancy and excitement surrounding all three of them.

Suddenly I remembered the cat. 'Oh no, Prowler,' I said. 'What's going to happen to him?'

'Oh not that bloody moggy,' groaned James.

'Jimmy!' I exclaimed, 'Don't you dare swear like that — and he's not what you called him.'

'You swear,' said James.

'I do not!' I exclaimed again, my face burning.

'Yes you do, yes you do!' joined in the other two.

'Shall I tell what you called Dad when he sent you up to the bookie on the corner four times last Saturday? It begins with "b" and ends with "d",' said Patrick.

'A bloody,' exclaimed Tim triumphantly. They all laughed. I was in tears yet again. What would Joan and Dennis think of me? But they were laughing too.

'Prowler's mine,' I said, wanting to change the subject, 'and he might get run over.'

'Hey, Miss,' it was James again. 'You know that moggy? He sleeps with her — he does — he puts his paws around her neck, and his whiskers next to her cheek, and he's probably bitten a nice juicy rat's head off!'

They all laughed, and prepared to go into more lengthy details, but Joan rescued me; though not before I'd kicked Timmy, the wrong one.

'Sorry, Tim,' I said, 'You can have my lucky bag.' But as he punched my arm, he said, 'I don't want it, it's a girl's!'

'Listen, children,' said Joan, 'one thing we ought to tell you is that Auntie Pam and Uncle Tom's little girl Marie is not very well, and she needs more rest than other children, but she is so excited that you'll be staying, that she's been allowed to wait up tonight.' I decided that Marie should have my lucky bag.

10

The following two weeks were probably the happiest we'd spent (except, of course, for missing Mummy and Gran so) since we'd gone to Southend two and a half years ago. They were certainly the most carefree I'd had in a long, long time. Auntie Pam and Uncle Tom were angels. Their house was new and lovely, with a swing and a small sand-pit in the garden. They had a record player with a radio too, which Uncle Tom explained was called a radiogram. This looked just like a piece of furniture, and I was delighted.

Auntie Pam would let me stay up later if Anna went to sleep without any trouble and would play Dickie Valentine singing 'All the Time and Everywhere'; it reminded me of Mummy, which made me feel happy and sad, both at the same time. Another favourite record was Doris Day's 'Secret Love', and it was when we were playing that one evening that I remembered who Joan reminded me of: it was Doris Day.

'Yes, you're right, she does,' said Auntie Pam. 'I bet she wishes she'd got her money, though.'

Uncle Tom made aeroplanes with the boys, out of balsa-wood, and they had great fun putting the stickers on and flying them across the room. One morning, as I was feeding Anna, I saw a robin on the garden fence; I called the boys and Marie, and we all looked in amazement. It was the first time the boys and I had seen a robin in our lives. I thought it was just a bird someone had dreamed up to put on Christmas cards and cakes!

Marie, the little girl, was pale, with fair curly hair, and was very pretty. She was going to be four on Christmas Eve. The boys had a room with twin beds and a camp-bed in it, overlooking the garden, and Uncle Tom drew up a rota so that they all got to sleep in the camp-bed. I had a bed all to myself, with a cot for Anna next to it, but most nights, after she's been to sleep for an hour or so, I would have to let the side down, and she'd crawl in next to me.

The memory of my father was beginning to fade, and it was only my middle finger that was bandaged now, the others were healed; but most nights I would cry for Mummy, Gran and Prowler. Some nights, if I couldn't sleep, my imagination would run away with me, and I would think of him telling a nurse or a priest of my immortal sins. On those nights the shadows on the trees outside would appear grotesque, like his long, bony hands beckoning when he wanted to whisper 'Murderer'. Sometimes, after such a night, I would be irritable with Anna and Marie who tended to squabble. Always it seemed that Anna had to give in to Marie.

I loved Auntie Pam; she had brown hair that was cut in a 'bubble-cut', big blue eyes, a rather long nose and a thin mouth. She never wore make-up, but she always looked fresh and nice. She was tall and slim. She taught me how to make coconut pyramids and other cakes. I loved to hoover the carpets, and Auntie Pam didn't have to send her washing to the bag-wash, but had a machine that washed the clothes, with a mangle on top with rollers that moved on their own. Sheets, pillow slips, shirts and towels would come back all ironed, in flat brown-wrapped packages delivered in a big white laundry van. This was a whole new world to me. They had a TV too, much smaller than ours, though we all agreed that we liked it better.

Every afternoon Marie would have to have a sleep, and Anna did too. Sometimes, if it was raining, we would play 'Hangman', or 'Ludo' or read comics. Auntie Pam introduced me to *Lorna Doone*, and it was many years before I could bring myself to read it all the way through. If the weather was fine, we'd walk to see the cows in the field nearby; and we were awestruck the first time we came across one or two of the year's remaining blackberries on a bush. We would pick them, and once having eaten them, and confirmed that they were the same as the ones you could get off the barrow in the market, we'd scare ourselves by saying that perhaps they weren't, but were poison. Uncle Tom laughed when Timmy came home one afternoon with what he'd spat out firmly clenched in his little palm, as he waited for confirmation that it wasn't poison, but was indeed a blackberry.

As the days went by, a fear began to grow in me that this wouldn't last forever. One day, as Anna and Marie were squabbling over some bricks, Auntie Pam ran across the room, and, snatching the bricks from a bewildered Anna, took them and laid them in Marie's hands. I felt the tears spring into my eyes, and glowered at Marie. I had always known that she was more important to her parents than we were, and now I realized that what I had been praying for — that Auntie Pam and Uncle Tom would come to love us so much that they wouldn't want us ever to leave, — not ever — was not to be.

I gathered Anna up in my arms and ran to the bedroom, rocking her to and fro. I sobbed, my salty tears wetting Anna's red, soft, downy hair. We were cold, and I got into bed with her. Then, as I sang 'Ma Curly Headed Babby' we drifted off to sleep, her fingers twirling my hair. Suddenly I was being shaken by the arm, and once again the old terror was back. In jumping up quickly, I had jolted Anna awake, and she began to cry.

'I'm sorry if I startled you, darling.' It was Auntie Pam. She took Anna in her arms and sat down on the bed. 'I'm sorry for what happened earlier, it wasn't very nice of me, I know. It's just that sometimes it gets too much for me. You see, Uncle Tom and I have only ever fostered one or two children in the past – but you are very special to us, you do believe that, don't you?'

I nodded. She didn't need to go on. We weren't any different, we were just another of 'them', just another group of faces in a picture – photos of children, boys and girls, black and white, littered the sitting room – only we *were* different, of course, there were five of us. Why, oh why, had I thought we'd got a chance this time? Bitterly I recalled Uncle Tom trying to take photos of the five of us with Marie, all squeezed up together round the sand-pit. I wondered where *those* photos would be placed? On the radiogram, perhaps?

' . . . and we've come to love you all very much. It will be as hard for us, and with Marie going into hospital it will hurt us . . . ' I didn't want to hear this. 'You'll come and spend some time with us next summer, won't you . . . '

I'd hoped I'd been nodding in the right places, but suddenly it didn't matter, even if I hadn't. I'd washed the floors, peeled potatoes and cleaned the grate, done the hoovering, put the washing in the machine and then through the 'magic mangle', used an electric iron – but I couldn't hold this against her because I'd enjoyed that part. She had even confided in me once that her own mother had died when she was nine and her father had replaced her with the original fairy-tale wicked stepmother when she was my age. I'd nearly confessed to her that evening about what my father had done to me and what they would do to me if they knew about Mummy's cause of death; I'd been so confident that she and Uncle Tom would protect me. And yet something had held me back, some sixth sense, and I thanked God now that it had.

The following day things seemed back to normal, but I sensed they were not. It was Uncle Tom who knocked on the door of my bedroom that night, just as Anna had crawled in beside me. 'Hello, young lady, I've come up to have a little chat. Auntie Pam is very tired and upset at the moment. She told you that Marie has to go back into the children's hospital next week; and although it's going to be a terrible wrench for us, your Daddy is out of hospital now, and everything is back to normal at home. I've spoken to the boys, and...'

So, everything was 'back to normal', was it?

'When?' I interrupted him. 'When do we have to go?'

'Well, dear, Joan and Dennis are calling at eleven on Friday morning. Your Daddy wanted you back earlier...'

So we had one more whole day; tomorrow was Thursday.

'...and so I thought it would be nice if I took you and the boys to the pictures in Welwyn tomorrow night, after we've got all the packing out of the way.'

'No, no thank you, Uncle Tom.' My throat felt constricted. 'I'll stay with Anna. The pictures make my head ache.'

'Well, when you come down in the summer, we'll go somewhere.' He bent and kissed me good night, and left the room. I was grateful that he'd gone. Once more Anna's gossamer hair was drenched with tears. Oh God, back to Dad! Things were back to normal, all right.

The next morning the big suitcase, and a small blue cardboard one given to us by Auntie Pam, lay open on her and Uncle Tom's bed as I passed. The atmosphere hung heavily around the house all day. Auntie Pam was busily ironing our clothes, and the boys had been given a cardboard box to put their comics and odds and ends in. They were giving me furtive glances as they went up the stairs at various times during the day, with clothes and shoes to lay on the bed next to the cases. I couldn't speak to Auntie Pam very easily, and couldn't bring myself to speak to little Marie at all!

The boys eventually went off to see a Bowery Boys film with Uncle Tom, and I made Anna a bottle of cocoa and a cup for myself, and went to bed. Anna had just fallen asleep, though I had made no attempt to put her in the cot (where Auntie Pam always insisted she should sleep), but held her close to me. I heard Auntie Pam come into the room, but feigned sleep, and at last she kissed my cheek, and then Anna's, releasing a long sigh as she did so. Then she left the room.

I heard the boys come back with Uncle Tom. They were recalling bits of the film, and there was much laughter. Uncle Tom told the boys not to be long over drinking their cocoa, and that the chocolate for Anna, Marie and myself was on the sideboard. Hearing the boys whispering in their room, with the occasional giggle, I longed to go in to them. We couldn't go back to our father, we just couldn't.

Perhaps we could all get up very early, 'borrow' some money from Auntie Pam's purse, and just take enough clothing to keep us warm, and enough food for the journey. I knew where the station was, it was a bit of a walk, but we had the push-chair. We could go back to London and find a bombed-out house somewhere – we'd played on bomb-sites all our lives, and we knew which ones were safe. We'd learned to improvise marvellously on the remains of people's lives and homes, and this time it would be for real!

Someone would have to go and collect Prowler. James and I could get paper rounds, and we wouldn't have to worry about veg and things, you could always pick up quite a lot of the stuff after the stalls had closed along the market. It was the only way. I could hear Uncle Tom and Auntie Pam talking softly in the next room. Give it a while and they'd be asleep, then I could creep into the boys' room with the 'plan'.

Anna woke me. She was wet, and I could hear Auntie Pam's voice downstairs. Oh God, I'd fallen asleep. I took Anna's nappy off and put it in the bucket in the bathroom. The boys were sitting, eating toast, and I put a nappy in the high chair for Anna to sit on. Breakfast, which had always been a noisy affair, had become a silent one, as I began to feed Anna her Farley's Rusks. After breakfast I dressed Anna and then myself – wondering whether I should leave behind the yellow pyjamas that Auntie Pam had given me. I decided to put them on top of the new brimming suitcases, along with Anna's nightie and sleeping bag. She could take them back herself if she wanted them.

The announcer on 'Housewives' Choice' was dedicating a record for someone in Welwyn, and I thought it might be for Auntie Pam. It wasn't – but I wondered briefly if it would have made any difference if I had written in for one for her. Probably not. Uncle Tom was being excessively cheerful (he'd taken the day off work). I began to wish that Joan and Dennis would come.

I went up to the bedroom to fetch Anna's toy lamb from the cot, and look around for anything else we'd left behind; suddenly I remembered the chiffon scarf down the side of the bed. I groped until I came across it. It was beginning to feel stiff and I held it to my nose again. The smell of 'Evening in Paris' still lingered – thank God I hadn't left it behind.

A car drew up outside, and Uncle Tom held the door open for Joan and Dennis to enter.

'Well, hello everyone,' boomed Dennis.

'Hello', we answered.

'You've all had a good time then. My! Look at the roses in your cheeks,' exclaimed Joan.

The four adults sat down and had coffee while the boys were taking advantage of their last playtime in the garden. I sat and read a book to Anna and Marie, so that I didn't have to look up or speak to any of them. Auntie Pam had made Anna a bottle for the journey, and there were sweets for us all, as well as the chocolate for Anna and myself for 'missing' the pictures.

Dennis and Uncle Tom were now organizing our suitcases and the box and assorted carrier bags. I didn't offer to help, but when they called the boys in from the front garden, I began to put Anna's siren suit on her. Suddenly it was time to go. Auntie Pam and Uncle Tom were kissing the boys and promising to see them next summer, and I stood with Anna on my hip as usual. Uncle Tom took her from me and threw her into the air, producing squeals of delight. Auntie Pam came and put her arms around me. 'I'll miss you, sweetheart,' she said. 'And me,' I answered. I bent and kissed Marie, and suddenly Auntie Pam was gone, into the kitchen, clutching Marie by the hand.

As Uncle Tom handed Anna back to me, he kissed me, and putting his arms right round us both, he said, 'It won't be long until the summer, and we'll have lots of fun, just you wait!'

'Thank you for everything,' I stammered gratefully, and was then ushered out to the car by Dennis.

'See you in the summer, Uncle Tom,' called the boys. Auntie Pam reappeared with Marie in her arms as we drove off. She was pressing a hanky against her mouth, just as I did with the pink scarf, and they waved until we turned the corner out of sight.

The journey back was a strange one. We had arrived in the dark, but now squares of grass and bare trees were on either side of the road. At one point we passed a pigsty and Dennis stopped the car so that we could look at the beasts which had only been alive for us all in books before. 'Pooh!' shouted one of the boys, and Patrick said, 'It's Anna's nappy!' 'It is not!' I answered. The boys were all laughing. They were trying to tell Joan and Dennis about the film, and before we knew it, we were back in familiar surroundings. My heart was pounding as the car came to a stop outside the Mansions.

11

Our father was waiting at the front door as we came down the communal passage-way, arms outstretched.

'Darlins', wonderful t'have yers all home safe and sound with me again.'

He kissed each one of us, and Joan and Dennis put our cases on my bed in the back room. It took two trips. I saw Joan wince as Daddy shook her hand.

'I don't know how to thank yers both,' he said to them. New cups and saucers were set out on the table, with new side plates. A plate with a doily on it held a heap of fancy cakes.

As we all made our way into the kitchen, I glimpsed a floral dress as it flitted back into the scullery. Gran! Gran was back! I put Anna on the floor, and almost collided with a woman with blond hair and black roots that had spread all round the top of her head like a skull cap. She had black eyebrows which swept upwards giving her an expression of permanent surprise. Her lips were painted scarlet, in a bow, and she exposed two badly chipped front teeth when she smiled.

' 'Ello luv,' she said.

'Hello,' I replied, unable to hide my disappointment.

'Nar, 'ow many are yer?' She started to count. 'Nine,' she concluded.

'No tea for the baby,' I said, 'she's got her bottle.'

'Right y'are, luv.' She pottered back into the scullery and returned bringing three more cups and saucers. Then she made a great ceremony of pouring the tea.

'Now then, chilluns,' he said, 'this is Mrs Sullivan.'

'Hello,' I said, for the second time, joining the others.

'Well, aren't they beautiful kids and no mistake, they're a credit to you.'

My father sat there, beaming. Anna seemed lost, sitting on the floor amongst the sea of legs, then suddenly Mrs Sullivan swooped on her.

'Jest look at this darlin' baby,' she cooed. Anna was having none of this. Arching her back, she screamed as hard as she could, trying desperately to wriggle out of the strange arms that held her. Quickly I held out my arms, and she came to me, her sobs subsiding.

'No, darlin'.' said Dad. 'Give her back to Mrs Sullivan. She'll have to get used to other people holdin' her, sure she will.'

The operation was repeated, and now Anna's cheeks were suffused with colour, her throat making rasping sounds. I didn't know what to do, but it was Joan who saved the situation, and Mrs Sullivan was as anxious to rid herself of Anna as Anna was to be rid of her.

'Let Caroline take her, Mr O'Farrell,' said Joan. 'The little one has seen so many changes, she's bound to be fretful.'

'Of course, of course. I wasn't thinkin'. An' please call me Terry, everyone does, yer know!'

'And I'm Ruby,' piped up the black and blond haired woman. 'Call me Auntie Ruby, eh kids? It's more friendly like!'

Back in my arms Anna was holding her scalding cheek into my neck, twirling her fingers around my hair. I got up with her.

'Is it all right if I find her a bottle?' I asked.

'Yes, of course, dear,' said Joan.

I pulled the heavy suitcases off the bed, and found the carrier bag with her bottle in it. I lay back on the bed with her until she fell asleep; I'd forgotten how cold and lumpy the thin mattress was. I began to open the suitcases, but thought it best to leave the unpacking until she woke up. Instead I went into the kitchen. I took a cake that was offered and drank the now-cold tea. Joan and Dennis were standing as if to go.

'This is what I mean,' my father said to them. 'Turn round, darlin'.' He'd got his hands on my shoulders. 'She's becomin' round-shouldered, her little body's growin' too, and it's worryin' me, her always having to hold the baby.'

'Don't worry, Mr O' — Terry, the baby's growing too and won't always need carrying around'.

'It's this,' he was tapping his chest. 'It grieves me to see her havin' to do so much wid der baby; they're their daddy's girls though, so they are, even if the little one's forgotten me for the moment.' He kissed my cheek. Maybe she *has* remembered you, I thought wryly.

'Well, we'll have to be going,' said Joan. 'One of us will pop in after the weekend. How many days are you doing, Mrs Sullivan?'

'Three full an' two 'arf,' said the colourful Ruby.

'Bye then,' said Dennis, touching my hair.

'Bye,' I called to them, wondering, not for the first time, if they were 'going out' together.

'I don't know how to thank yers,' Dad repeated, as they made their way up the hall. The boys had gone out (they hadn't wasted much time). I began helping Ruby to clear the table.

''Ave a nice time?' she asked.

'Yes, thank you,' I replied, thinking, why couldn't it have been Gran?

Ruby was very slim, but her legs were totally without shape and her feet seemed to be engulfed somewhere in high strapped shoes.

'I'll go and start unpacking,' I said. He was still at the front door, giving his undying gratitude to Joan and Dennis as I slipped into the bedroom, and started unpacking all our things. I stiffened as I heard him come into the room.

'Now mind the boys do their fair share of puttin' away, darlin'.' he said. Thankfully I heard him disappear down the hall. I brought Anna's nappies and clothes through and put them in the kitchen cupboard, together with the two towels. I also put all the boys' things away. There had been three parcels inside a carrier, one with the boys' names on, one for me, and one for Anna. They all said, *With lots of love, Auntie Pam, Uncle Tom and Marie.* I opened mine and found it contained a white petticoat with lace round it, and a red tartan kilt.

Dad was in the kitchen, talking to Ruby, when the boys came back in. I heard them coming up the hall.

'There's a present for you from Auntie Pam and Uncle Tom.' Quickly they tore open the package. It held a 'blow football' game and scarf each.

'Thanks for helping me put your bloody things away,' I said, sarcastically.

'Don't start,' said James.

'Caroline,' I heard him call from the kitchen, 'go and get five pound of potatoes and a tin of processed peas. Auntie Ruby brought some sausages.'

I went to the stall where Mummy had always bought the vegetables, and gave only the barest information when the man asked why he hadn't seen us, and what had happened 'in there' — he pointed towards the Mansions.

As I was coming through the back yard, I saw a cat sitting on a coal shed. It was Prowler. 'Oh Prowler,' I said, 'come on, boy.' Prowl, prowl — in one leap he was winding himself around my legs. He followed me into the kitchen, where I put the shopping on the table.

'The cat's had some food,' my father said.

'Oh thanks Dad.' I was very grateful.

Ruby was punching holes in the sausages as I took the potatoes through.

'Leave 'em there, luv. Auntie Rube'll have yer dinner ready soon.' The boys had their game out on the kitchen table, and Timmy was trying to put a player into its base. The boys were obviously delighted with the game, and had just put together the last goal net as Ruby came through with the kitchen knives and forks.

'Clear the table fer yer Auntie Rube, boys.' A cigarette was hanging from her mouth and the ash dropped into the box. James glared. I laid the table, and presently Ruby came through with five plates of sausage, mash and peas.

'Sorry about the bangers. When they're bran, they're dun, and when they're black, they're buggered — trouble is, they always get buggered with yer Auntie Rube.' She laughed and went into the scullery. 'I'll bring yours after, Terry,' she called to him. 'I got yer a little bit of steak.'

She came in with cups of tea as I was wondering how I was going to get rid of the grit from my charcoaled sausage, and the boys began to titter, but I gave them a warning look. He was sitting in the rocking-chair, reading the paper, when I heard Anna cry.

'I'll get her,' he said, gently pushing me back into my chair. Anna was screaming as she came back through the door in his arms. This time he plonked her on my lap. After the meal, Ruby asked Dad if I could manage to take the sheets and things to the bag-wash.

'Yes, sure she can, as long as it's not too heavy now.'

I put on our coats, and James offered to come too.

'Who's that old doll?' he asked.

'I don't know,' I told him truthfully.

'Did you see her teeth?'

'Yes, they're horrible,' I said.

'I reckon she got them smashed up trying to eat her bloody cooking,' said James, doubling up with laughter. I joined in, and Anna bounced about on top of the bag-wash, laughing too.

'He's being all right, though, isn't he?'

'So far, Jimmy, so far. I thought it was Gran back,' I said.

'Christ, you going blind?' He started laughing again. Do you think he'll let us in the front room now?'

'I don't know, Jimmy, you *never* know with him.'

When we got back, he was sitting at the table, drinking tea. Ruby had kicked her shoes off, and was holding forth. 'Well, Terry, they ain't always right. Look at TB fr'instance, lost three of 'er kids wiv it me mother did, an' look at it now, they got a cure, luv. Sometimes I don't think there's no God up there, I knows yer Catholic an' I don't wanna be speakin' out of turn, but when I looks at a 'andsome man like you, bein' left wiv these youn 'uns. Well, I jest can't 'elp wonderin'. Yer in pain, luv, yer go an' 'ave a lie down an' I'll bring yer a cuppa in a couple a hours.'

Prowler was sitting under the table, making crunching noises. Looking up, Ruby said to Dad, ' 'E's having a bit of a treat — 'e likes 'is steak well done, your cat does.'

'That's her pride and joy, Ruby, so it is. Her mother bought him for her birthday, didn't she, darlin'?'

I nodded.

'Lovely markings 'e's got, Terry, yer can see that they've got tigers for their ancestors.'

Dad stood up and suddenly produced two half-crowns. 'We'll be needing some more bread and a cake, Ruby,' he said. He turned to me. 'You'll go for it, darlin'?'

'Yes, Dad.'

He was speaking breathlessly now, and tapping his chest, he suddenly reached across and, holding Ruby's wrist, said quietly, 'Ruby, don't let yers faith be shaken — the Holy Mother has sent yer to us.'

'Yer go in fer a nap now, Terry, 'fore yer 'ave me in tears,' she said, sniffing.

'Ruby, you're a darlin', give the chilluns the change for some sweets.' He pointed to the two half-crowns on the table, and, touching James's hair, he left the room. We heard him unlock the front bedroom and close the door. Patrick and Timmy were playing blow football in our bedroom.

'Can I help?' I asked Ruby.

'We'll get the dishes done an' yer can go round the bakers an' get a split tin and a custard tart – a big 'un, mind,' she said to James. 'Get a pound of broken biscuits too, luv.'

James walked out of the back door. When he came back, she put the change in my hand and took another sixpence from her purse. ' 'Ere you are. Go an' get some sweets. Take the other two wiv yer, so's yer Dad can get some sleep.'

I'd opened a tin of beans and was cutting slices of bread. Ruby was ironing Dad's shirts on the kitchen table.

'Pity yer dad didn't get a 'lectric iron when he was in the money, and that bloody old cooker scares me 'arf to death. But still, it'd be just like 'im to get yer mum embalmed an' all. – Bought 'er a private plot up the cemetery an' all, took 'im all 'is compensation money, it did.'

She seemed to know an awful lot about us, and I felt angry, but all I said was, 'What's embalmed mean?'

'Well, it's something the undertakers do, ta keep yer body preserved for years and years, so if they was to dig yer Mum up in about fifty years or so, she'd look jest the same as when she died.'

This idea terrified me, and I ran into the back room, took out the chiffon scarf from the back of my drawer, and deeply inhaled. 'Come back, Mummy,' I whispered into it. I noticed the package addressed to Anna on the floor, and picking it up, we both unwrapped it. Inside there was a pink, knitted cardigan and some new bricks. Anna sat on the half-moon rug in front of the fire, building them up and knocking them down again. I'd shown Ruby how toast was made on our gas stove – in fact it had come as a great surprise to me when Auntie Pam's toast was a golden-brown colour all over. Our grill had never worked in my memory, and as I turned the rings on low, and put the toast on each ring and quickly turned them over, there were sporadic burnt bits on the bread, and it was done. I turned the beans into an old enamel saucepan, and went to fetch the boys. They were playing on a bomb-site.

'Liars, bleedin' liars,' Ronnie Nelson was shouting at them.

'We were, weren't we, chased by a bull?' James asked, opening his eyes wide, daring me to deny this 'fact'.

'Yes, we were, and your tea's ready, you lot,' I said to all three of them.

'She wearing red drawers then?' said Pete Matthews, squealing at his joke as he kicked an old piece of mangle about.

'You didn't believe how big our "telly" was, did you?' piped up Patrick, 'but you couldn't believe your eyes when you saw it.'

'An' we got a maid now, so put that in your pipe and smoke it!'

'Fuckin' liar,' shouted Ronnie Nelson.

Quickly I ushered the three of them into the flat.

'Is he up yet?' asked James.

'No,' I replied, but he was.

'Come on, chilluns, wash yers hands – look at the lovely tea yer Auntie Ruby has made yers.' She smiled, and said, as she was pouring the tea. 'I'll put yer shirts away, Terry luv.'

'No, Ruby, I'll do that, yers sit down an' have some tea.'

It was with some satisfaction that I saw her pull a face – she too was not allowed into the back bedroom. The Queen was dead, but there was to be no succession yet! During the next two weeks things ran fairly smoothly; some days he'd give me the bus fare to take Anna to nursery, but mostly we walked there through the freezing streets. Prowler was allowed in at night, and it looked as if things were going to be OK. I'd still go to the bag-wash and to Harvey's coal yard for fourteen pounds of 'slack' and Ruby had given up the ironing after she'd burnt one of his collars.

But my sleep was unbroken. Sometimes, when I came back from school and nursery, Ruby would be there on her two afternoons off, and I'd have to get some bread and jam for tea and some broken biscuits if he had enough money. The kitchen would be hazy with smoke and the ashtrays full to over-flowing. Sometimes this situation would present itself on the days when she *should* be working through, but Dad was in a much more reasonable frame of mind, so it seemed a small price to pay.

We came home one day and he gave us each a letter from Auntie Pam and Uncle Tom. That night I sat and wrote a long letter to them, telling them how much we all missed them. I wanted to take out some sort of insurance against them ever forgetting us. We never heard from them again, and just before Christmas, Dad told us that Joan had come and said that little Marie had died. I felt very sad, but I wondered too if, with Marie gone, we stood a better chance of going back to them; so I wrote again, but still received no reply.

12

One afternoon I hurried home to find the table spread with fish-paste sandwiches and cakes. Dad seemed in a good mood, and he even made a few jokes as he poured our tea. After tea he asked the boys to do the washing up and sent me to Dr Scanlon's for a prescription. When I came back, the boys were in their pyjamas, and there were some crisps and a bottle of Tizer on the kitchen table, with a bar of chocolate for Anna. I was a bit perplexed. Anna was shuffling about in her sleeping bag like a little mandarin, so I picked her up and put her nappy on properly.

'Now, darlins',' he said, 'I want you to be good tonight for yer Daddy, and give yer sister some peace to do her homework.' Homework! I was so far behind that everything I'd written in my books was the work of a couple of girls who had remained friends with me following the incident when he'd gone up to the school. I had very little in common with my peers. I never went swimming after school, or to the Youth Club they talked about. They'd even given up asking me. Everyone had started their periods and had had their ears pierced; which, to me, was the greater status symbol, I wasn't sure, but both *were* symbols, and I'd had neither.

'Daddy's got to go to a meeting, and I won't be back late. Just tuck in,' he gestured towards the Tizer and the crisps, 'an' go to bed when yer sister tells yer. I'm puttin' her in charge of yers.'

We couldn't wait for him to go, and he seemed to take ages shaving. The boys stayed up until nine o'clock, and Anna, who'd grizzled all night, chewing on a finger, one cheek highly flushed, eventually went off at about ten, after I'd mixed a Steedman's Powder in a little milk and sugar on a spoon. She was cutting her back teeth.

I lay down on the bed with her, and the next thing I was being gently shaken. He didn't have the torch, but I could smell rum on his breath; instantly alert, I jumped out of bed and he pulled me, still gently, towards the bright light of the kitchen. I'd fallen asleep in my school uniform, and looked down in dismay at the creased green tunic.

'Sit down , darlin',' he said. His eyes were very bright, and very, very blue,and his black hair, always combed so carefully back with Brylcreem, had a stray lock hanging down which made him look different. I was growing more apprehensive as I sat at the kitchen table opposite him.

'Somethin' wonderful's happened, darlin','he said, unscrewing the top of one of the two bottles of beer that were on the table. 'Get Daddy a glass, there's a good, good girl yers are.'

I brought a glass and put it in front of him. 'An' one fer yerself, darlin', sure, c'mon now.'

I went and fetched a cup, and he poured some of the beer into it. 'Good health, darlin', he raised his glass. 'Drink up, 'tis full of iron.'

I tasted the bitter brew, and tried not to screw my face up too much. 'It's nice,' I said.

'Now don't be getting a liking for the stuff,' he laughed, and lit another Player. 'This is our secret, what I'm goin' to be tellin' yers, OK?''

I nodded.

'We've got another little secret, you and I, sure we have, but it won't be passin' yer Daddy's lips – oh no!'

I flushed, and wriggled nervously in my seat. The familiar throb was in my spine.

'I've been to what they call a Spiritualist Meeting.' This meant nothing to me. I just sat and stared. 'It's called a seance.'

Still nothing. 'It – well, if yers are well disposed, it can bring back yer loved one from the dead.'

My spine had now locked painfully. I wanted to go to the toilet and felt my knickers become a little damp. I sat on my hand, putting pressure on my offending bladder, hoping to staunch the flow.

'Drink up darlin'.' I put the cup to my lips and pretended to drink.

'Darlin', our Holy Mother Church doesn't agree to these things at all — though 'tis only a matter of time before they will, sure they will. I went to the meetin' wid someone I'd not seen for years. Powerful good it did him too! I went to a big house, near Hampstead it was, an' when they asked to take my overcoat, I thought, "yers not goin' to have that an' be goin through me pockets for information", so I kept it on, sure I did, checkin' the pockets, makin' sure everythin' was still there. I was introduced to some fine people, fine people. Two ladies and the one they called the medium, nicely spoken like yer Mammy, God rest her, and some fine fellas were there too.'

My fear was growing. He filled his glass and lit another cigarette, his eyelids drooping. 'We was all sittin' round a large fine polished table, and the medium says a prayer, an' asks us all to join hands which we did. After a minute or two she says, "George, is there a George here? Please answer." "Yes," says a fella with a baldy head. "I have a Betty — no, a Beattie — yes, yes, I understand," she says to the dead person now. "She wants yer to know that she's very happy and has met her mother again — and I have an Albert or Alfred here, do you know who this is, George?" "Yes," says George. He's across the table from me and I can see his hands are shakin'. "It's my brother Fred," says this George. "Well, he says to tell you he's reunited with Elsie, and that he's watching over you from the other side." "Oh my God," says this George, "Can you get Beattie back again?" "I'm so sorry, she's fading, no, she's gone."

'Well then she goes on to one of the ladies, who she says is called Isabel. The lady agrees wid her, an' she tells her about a fall she had in the snow and broke her leg — this poor lady is overcome. 'Tis her husband Charles, the medium tells her. Now, listen to this will yers, darlin',' and he drained the first bottle into his glass. He was chain-smoking now. 'She seems to be talking to herself again, an' then she says. "Is there a Thomas here?" No one answers. "Or a Tim?" I naturally thought of little Timmy — and then, blessed if she doesn't say, sure she does, "Or a Terence perhaps?" I wasn't going to answer, and then the poor woman starts holdin' her head. "I'm feelin' great pain in my head, please take it away," she says t'the spirit on the other side. "I have a dark young woman here for Terence, her name is Eileen or Irene?" "It's Irene," I find myself telling her. "She says she's free of pain now, and she loves you, she brings you red roses and says the month of June is important to you both." "It is, sure it is," I tell her. I'm sorry, darlin'.' he said as he took his hanky out, wiping the tears away from his cheeks, and reaching across to unscrew the other bottle.

I was cold, very cold, but I knew I mustn't move. 'She says to tell you she loves you and the babies, and she forgives . . . ' he broke off, his eyes once again seeming to pierce my very soul. My bladder was bursting, and I fidgeted.

'Still!' he shouted, 'Be still! She tells me there will be important papers to sign, and I must sign them. Then the medium says "She tells me she will come back again soon, she is fadin' now." She calls on someone else who answers to his name. We had a cup of coffee afterwards. So comfortin' to know there's a life hereafter . . . '

'Can I go to the . . . '

'Sit down for Jesus' sake.' I sat. 'Do yers see, darlin', how could anyone in the room have known our names, the terrible pains in the head.'

He spilled beer on to the table cloth. I didn't move.

'Yers know her favourite flowers was red roses, it was our song. "Red Roses for a Blue Lady." It was the month of June we met, yers didn't know that now, did yers?' No, sure yers didn't. She's here in this house, I can feel her, she's in this very room I'm tellin' yers.'

I looked around, petrified, but I could see nothing.

'Don't yers be lookin' afraid now, she loves yers an' she's forgiven yers for what yer did.'

I felt my navy blue school knickers become a warm pulp beneath me.

'She forgives yers, and I forgive yers.' He poured the last inch of beer into his glass. Softly he started singing . . . 'I want some red roses for a blue lady, Mr Florist take my order please, we had a silly quarrel the other day, I hope these pretty flowers take her blues away . . . wrap up some red roses . . . ' He started sobbing, ugly, uncontrollable sobs, resting his head on his arm.

The nightmare was back – though it had taken on a different form, but maybe this was worse. I couldn't move; urine had fallen down the side of the chair and made puddles on the floor. He began to snore, softly, but I waited. His cigarette was burning between his fingers. Oh God, please don't let him wake up! Gingerly I took the cigarette from him, and stood up; throwing the cigarette end into the dying embers, I walked slowly past him into the scullery.

There was a little water in the kettle, and I put it into the all-purpose bowl. Then I began to take off my sopping socks and knickers, and washed myself down with Lifebuoy soap, after which I put the socks and knickers into the bowl of soapy water and wrung them out. Creeping back out, I hung them on the fire-guard to dry.

The back of my tunic was clinging to my buttocks like wet ice as I crept along the passage way. Anna stirred as I opened my drawer and retrieved an old blue jumper and the kilt Auntie Pam had given me. I put on some ankle socks and plimsolls, and lay down beside Anna, fully clothed. Then I remembered that I hadn't mopped up the chair and floor.

Suddenly I heard a movement in the kitchen. Oh please don't let him come back! In the dark my heart pounded as I heard a bottle fall and break, then more movement, and I heard the lock turn on the front bedroom door. I'd wait until I heard him snore a hundred times, I thought, and then get up. – Once again a lock was being turned. Oh no, I prayed. His footsteps were coming up the hallway, and I heard him swear as he bumped into the toilet door, then the sound of him urinating, which seemed to go on for an eternity. He moved off, back down to the bedroom again, and in about five minutes his snores could be heard throughout the flat.

I climbed swiftly out of bed. The kitchen light was on, and everything was as I had left it, except that one of the beer bottles had rolled onto the floor and smashed. I picked up the larger pieces of brown glass and threw them in the dustbin, sweeping up the rest with the dustpan and brush. Then I pulled the big metal fire-guard away from the hearth and took the ashpan out, leaving it on the hearthstone to cool. Next, putting the kettle on, I washed the chair and floor with a piece of my 'nosebleed' sheeting. After that I emptied the contents of the dustpan and the ashtray into the ashpan in the hearth, and took that out to the dustbin too.

Slowly I started to put large cinders on the fire and then pieces of coal, and held a newspaper over the opening. After a few minutes the paper began to scorch. Thank God, the fire was taking. Something had gone right. Creeping back to the bedroom I brought my tunic through, then took the ironing sheet from the cupboard and spread it on the table. I also took the iron from the cupboard, and set it on a low gas. Reaching behind an old tin at the back of the cabinet, I took out a sachet of Nescafé, poured hot water on it in the cup, and added some sterilized milk and saccharins. I sat rocking in Mummy's chair. Tomorrow I would look up the meaning of the words 'spiritualist' and 'medium' in the dictionary. I shuddered, remembering this latest turn of events.

Taking one of Dad's hankies, I rinsed it through, and then ironed the three pleats into place in the front of my tunic, and the rest of the tunic dry; as I ironed, the stench of urine and heat in the room became suffocating. Quickly I threw up the bottom window — I was not afraid of what was without, it was what was within that frightened me. Panicking now, I realized that I wouldn't be able to iron the boys' shirts because of the smell, and I dumped the ironing sheet and Dad's hankie into the bag-wash bag. The smell subsided.

Even the odour of the Lifebuoy soap on my pants and socks was growing fainter now. I wondered if it was worth going to bed. It seemed ages ago that I had heard the Express Dairy milkman rattle his bottles up the hall. I tried to tune the wireless, but after picking up snatches of foreign stations and music, I gave up trying to get the Light Programme or Home Service. Then I went outside, and could just make out the time from the clock on the Northern Polytechnic building; it said 6.35 a.m.

There were lots of buses and people about. Outside the front door I picked up the bottle of sterilized milk and the bottle of pasteurized milk, and made my way through the back yard and in again. I put a pan of water on the gas stove, added a little of yesterday's milk, threw in two cupfuls of Quaker Oats and a teaspoon of salt, and put it on a low heat. Anna was coming up the hall. 'Dink, Mummy Caroo, dink,' she said, pointing at her bottle, and I put some orange juice in it for her, and sat her in Mummy's chair. She smiled up at me while greedily sucking at the bottle. I gave the porridge a stir, and put the gas on full under the kettle.

'Going to get the boys,' I said. 'Stay there, baby.' Anna sat silently rocking. I went into the back bedroom. 'Jimmy, Jimmy, wake up! I demanded. 'Wake the others up — quietly — he's started again.'

'Oh fuck,' said James.

One by one they traipsed through the kitchen, and I warned, 'Mind the floor, he smashed a beer bottle last night.'

'On you?' asked Patrick.

'No, don't be daft. On the floor. I hope your shirts'll last another day, I was too tired to iron them.' I brought their tea and porridge through.

I put some sugar on their porridge and saccharins in the tea.

'Take his in, Jimmy,' I said.

'Oh great, bloody great,' he protested, but he took it in.

'Got enough arsenic in there?' asked Patrick. Timmy giggled. James came back, carrying the cup. 'No answer – he's still pissed!'

'Jimmy, your language!' I said. Anna was having her nappy changed, and was saying, 'P . . . ss . . . t, p . . . ss . . . t!' The boys fell about laughing.

'What a pong,' said Timmy, as the offending nappy came off.

'What a bloody waft to try to eat your breakfast through!' complained James.

'She can't help it if her wee-wee's strong, can you?' I smiled at her.

'We could always bottle it and sell it as smelling salts,' cracked one of the boys.

Patrick went to take his breakfast dishes out to the scullery, and I asked him to bring the zinc powder in. After liberally dowsing Anna with the powder, I finished dressing her and fed her her porridge.

'What's he started again for?' whispered James.

'I'll tell you on your own.' I glanced at the other two. 'Jimmy, would you take the washing up to the bag-wash? It opens at eight o'clock. The bag's heavy, so you'll have to use the push-chair.'

'I'm not pushing a bloody push-chair,' said James, indignantly. 'Anyway, that's another of that Ruby's jobs.'

'Please Jimmy,' I said, putting Anna's nappy and her nightie at the bottom of the bag. 'He's kept me awake all night again, I promise I'll tell you all about it.'

'OK,' James relented. 'Me and Patrick will take it, but it's that old cow's job.'

I left Anna in the rocking-chair looking at a cloth book, and went into the back bedroom. As I was putting on yesterday's blouse and the offending tunic, I glanced over at the other bed. Timmy was lying in it, fully clothed.

'What's the matter, Tim? Aren't you very well?' I went over to him. He was sobbing. 'I want my mummy,' he cried. 'I want my mummy.'

'Oh Timmy, I know, but Mummy's in Heaven, and she's watching over us.' (I shuddered as I remembered last night.) I held him close and rocked him gently. 'Here,' I said, pulling a threepenny bit from under my pillow, 'Don't tell the others.'

He smiled, trying to wipe away his tears. It wasn't very long ago that he was everybody's baby – though it seemed light years away.

'Now, go in with Anna while I finish getting dressed too.

13

That day during the mid-morning break, I went into the school library and took down an Oxford English Dictionary from the shelf, thumbing through it quickly until I read the following:

spiritualism – *belief that departed spirits communicate with the living.*

medium – middle position, intermediary, *one through whom others seek to communicate with dead spirits.*

Oh Holy Mother! He hadn't been lying – everything he had said was true. I went to the nurse after lunch, saying I'd vomited – which I had. I fell asleep while I was waiting, and sat bolt upright as my arm was shaken.

'Sorry, Nurse,' I said. 'Have afternoon classes started?'

'They've been and gone, my love. It's home time, and I think you should go and see your own doctor. Who is he, by the way?'

'Dr Scanlon.'

'Oh, he's a good man. You look a bit peaky to me, dear. Now, off you pop.'

My father began going out to these spiritualist meetings quite frequently during the next week or so. Some nights he'd be angry if he hadn't heard from the 'other side', as he called it. At other times that terrible shaking of the arm would arouse me, but he didn't shine the torch any more. It was on these nights that I would trail behind him down the freezing hallway, while he would tell me excitedly how he'd been called, always embellishing my mother's messages with things that no one on God's earth except the two of them could have known.

By now we too were being named by the medium, and even Prowler was among the names she'd given him. What more proof could we want? And no longer would he hint at her forgiveness, now she had actually forgiven me my 'crime'. Sometimes, if Ruby wasn't there, we would listen at the bedroom door as he carried on seemingly lucid conversations with our mother; she was obviously responding by asking him certain questions too, to which he could be heard giving long answers or explanations.

When I'd told James where Dad was going, and the things he was coming home and waking me to tell me (omitting, of course, her forgiveness of my 'crime'), he hadn't believed me. One night, however, he'd crept down the hallway himself, and listened. When I eventually got back into bed in the early hours, James said, 'Caroline, I was listening to him tonight. What does he mean, she's here in the house, does he mean she's haunting us?'

'That's what he says, but you know Mummy never believed in ghosts.'

'No, she didn't, but she couldn't have been sure there weren't any, could she?'

'I suppose not,' I said.

'What does he mean by the "other side"?'

'Heaven.'

'Oh. If she appears, like he said she's going to, will you be scared?'

'No,' I said.

'Why not?' persisted James.

'Because I don't believe him,' I said. But I *was* scared, and I *did* believe him.

Christmas was nearly upon us; it had been nagging at me since we'd come back from Auntie Pam and Uncle Tom's, which was when all the shop windows had started to come alight. We'd usually been up to Regent Street by now, and seen the lights. We did have about a dozen paper chains, and a couple of silver bells and some tarnished tinsel. But even the fairy, which we had had since I could remember, had lost her wings and looked tatty and grey. With no tree to put her on, a big question mark about Christmas hung over all of us – especially over me, it seemed, since the boys would always be asking me to ask *him*!

About two days after we broke up for the Christmas holidays, Ruby was sitting in front of the fire with Dad, shoes off, drinking a cup of tea that I'd made for them both. She jumped up like a scalded cat as Joan put her head around the kitchen door.

'Come in, come in, it's good to see you,' said my father. 'Now, will yer sit down and have a cup of tea for goodness' sake. Ruby, make Miss Bowden a cup too, will yers?'

Ruby went out into the scullery, clinking crockery about, and quickly I picked Anna up from the rug where she had been playing with her bricks. This was the first time I'd seen Joan since we arrived back from the country, and I was seized with such anger against her that I wanted to run away. I began to walk out of the room.

'Hey, hey, hey, an' where've yer good manners gone, young lady? Yer've forgotten to say "good morning" to Miss Bowden.'

'Good morning,' I mumbled.

'I'm sorry it's been such a long time since I've seen you, Caroline. I *have* called, but I haven't always found anyone at home, and at other times I've just had a word with Daddy and Mrs Sullivan. But I came as soon as I could, and I promise I'll try and fit in some evening visits now and again. Am I forgiven?'

'Now put the baby back down, for Heaven's sake, darlin'.'

I put Anna back on the floor.

'She's looking very tired, Mr – I mean, Terry.'

They both laughed.

'Yes, I must admit to being a bit worried, she's been havin', an awful lot of these nose bleeds of hers lately. Sometimes we've been up 'til all hours, putting the cold keys down the back, cold water on the neck – haven't we?'

I nodded. It was with a strange fascination that I would listen to his lies as they tripped so easily off his tongue.

'Sometimes I've been near t'gettin' the Doc out, but she won't let me.'

'I think it would be an idea if Dr Scanlon does see her, Terry. She's very pale.'

'Yes, I'll take her up myself, sure I will.'

Ruby tottered in, the shoe straps not done up over her bulging feet – and I hoped that she'd trip up!

'Well then, thank you, Mrs Sullivan. – What's Father Christmas bringing for little Anna?' she asked, leaning forward to speak to her. Anna looked up at her, waving a brick. Suddenly a shudder ran through me. I knew I couldn't stop myself – just as I'd known this day would come.

'We haven't got a tree or decorations, presents or anything,' I wailed, running from the room. The boys, in the bedroom, looked up at me with differing expressions, fear, awe, admiration, it was all there.

'Oh Jesus Christ, what'd you go and say that for?'

'Did you hear me then?' I rasped.

'They must have heard you in the bloody Tower!' said James. 'But why did you say it then, especially in front of the Welfare.'

'Oh, 'cos it's fucking true!' I cried.

'You're as good as dead,' said James, comfortingly.

'I know, I know!'

The door opened slowly. It was Ruby. 'Yer fer it, my gel, after all that man's done for yer.' More words of succour. 'Come on, yer buggers, on the other bed while I make this 'un.'

I could hear Anna crying; Ruby was tucking the sheet in against the wall. A crooked black seam ran up the back of her shapeless legs; as she bent over, black suspenders sunk into the folds of insipid flesh and black lace knickers could just be seen. James was trying to aim some peas at this spectacle with his blow football tube, while the other two boys were laughing hysterically.

I could hear Anna again, and was just going in to see to her when Ruby rounded on me. 'Don't you go in there, Miss, yer've caused enough bloody trouble for that poor Dad o' yours. That woman wants to talk to him "in private".'

Straightening herself up, she took her purse out of the front of her apron. ' 'Ere, go and get five pounds of spuds, 'arf a dozen eggs an' a nice pair o' kippers for yer Dad, and I wants ten Woodies an' ten Players. Yer can 'ave tuppence each – not that yer deserve it, yer ungrateful little buggers.' Ruby handed me a ten shilling note. I kept my tuppence in my pocket' (I'd get a sachet of Nescafé later), then went out.

'You get along in there, madam,' she sneered, as I came back and went straight into the bedroom. 'They wants t'speak t'you, an' I can't say I'm surprised.' I put the purchases on the bed. 'Git those bloody kippers out of 'ere an' take 'em through.'

My heart beating fast, I made my way down the hall. Joan was still there.

Anna had fallen asleep on the rug, bottle in her mouth.

'Come on in, darlin',' he called.

'I'm sorry.' I hung my head.

'Now, there's nothing to be sorry for, my sweet, yers are bound to be missin' yer Mammy, yer first Christmas widout her. We understand – and I've not got around to things as I should have. I know yer Mammy made Christmas very special, and I'll have to try, sure I will. It's what she would have wanted. Now, if you'll ask Auntie Ruby to pop in?'

Joan stood up. 'I'll be back to see you all on Thursday morning, I promise.'

'Wonderful,' he said. With that I picked Anna up, and shushing the boys as I went into the bedroom, I put her in our bed, telling Ruby, 'You're wanted.' For a moment she looked flustered, and I felt pleased. She lumbered out of the room, saying she'd 'bleedin' near froze' in there. Then Dad's footsteps were striding down the hallway after her, as he said his twentieth goodbye to Joan, and the next thing we saw was Ruby, passing the window as she shuffled through the back yard.

Now my father was calling us. We scuttled out of the room; I picked up the potatoes and eggs and cigarettes.

'If he goes to hit you, run for it,' advised James quietly.

'Now, darlins', yers all gonna be very busy chilluns. Where's Dad's girl?' He handed me an envelope. 'Take that up to Harvey's coal yard, and give it t'the man himself.'

I went to get the old leather bag. 'No need for that, darlin' ' he called. I was puzzled, and even wondered if it was some sort of trick as I stopped to catch my breath outside the yard. There was no one waiting at the big scales, so I took the letter straight to Mr Harvey in his little office, and he opened the envelope.

'Right you are, dearie,' he told me. 'Tell 'em it'll be Wednesday, can't do it no sooner, not with Christmas nearly here.'

Running back home I felt that familiar throb in my spine as I heard the boys and Anna screaming. But they weren't screaming, they were all laughing. Each one of the boys was brandishing a pound note in his hand – even Anna had a ten shilling note in hers, and was shrieking as she turned herself around and around before falling with a bump onto the floor. She was so giddy that James had to pick her up. I just stood and gaped.

Dad was tickling Timmy, and James was saying, 'Dad, Dad, it's better like this, it makes it more exciting.'

'Yeah, thanks, Dad,' said Patrick. Timmy looked at me as Dad swung him back down to the floor.

'Look, Caroline, look what Daddy gave us, for paper chains and candles and crackers and a tree and . . . '

'Oh thanks, Daddy!' I went up and kissed him.

'Thought yer Daddy had forgot, did yers?' he said to me. Then, 'Go help Auntie Ruby with yers dinner.'

At once I went into the scullery, where Ruby had just dished everything up. Quickly I laid the table and cut some bread and butter. Ruby came in and poured the teas, and I filled Anna's bottle with tea, then sat her in her high chair and began to feed her.

'Yer'll get no thanks for it, Terry,' Ruby called from the scullery. Dad raised his eyes to the heavens, and we all laughed conspiratorially. Even Ruby's sulks could not shake off the excitement that pervaded the room that day. Suddenly Dad got up from his chair, switched on the wireless, and immediately 'Rudolph the Red-nosed Reindeer' filled the room.

'See, yer Daddy's a magic man!' We all laughed and clapped.

Ruby began throwing YoYo biscuits at us all round the table, as if she were feeding crumbs to the birds. Still sniffing, and with her usual Woodbine hanging wetly from the corner of her mouth, she said, 'If yer wouldn't mind getting out as soon as yer can, I want yer Dad an' me t'ave a bit o' grub, so yer can all clear orf!' Once again he raised his eyes to the ceiling, and even told us the kippers would be burnt to the size of a sprat by the time Ruby had cooked them!

I gave a quick wipe to the other four faces, and to my own with the same flannel, then we all combed our hair, and made it out of the door in record time. Anna gave up the ten shilling note in exchange for a penny. As we began the long walk to Woolworths, we passed the shops and the boys said, 'I'm having that, and that, and that, and that . . . ' at each new toyshop or newsagent's window that we passed.

It was dark as we made our way back for our last and most important call — the tree. James was doing a jig, and the other boys were laughing at him as we made our way towards the market stalls. We were thrilled with our purchases

– tinsel, silver, green and red glass balls, cotton wool and glitter, paper chains and two pull-out decorations. James was holding a box of red and silver crackers and we kept taking them out of the bag – they seemed, in a way, more magical than anything. Anna was holding the new fairy doll very gently and talking to her. I had the tree candles in my pocket.

As we passed Forrester's, we gazed into the window, as we had done every day, at the snow-house in the display. It had cardboard windows with children peeping out of each curtained space, and a wreath of holly on the red front door, but the final touch of magic was the cotton-wool roof, covered in frost-like glitter, with a cardboard 'brick' chimney peeping through. One year we'd had a house like that, and it was opened after tea on Christmas night; my gift had been a beautiful hair-slide.

'Wish we could have that,' said Timmy.

'So do I,' I agreed, 'but we've only got one pound, and a couple of shillings change, and we've got to get the tree first – *and* we'll have to give him some change!'

Eventually we came to our veg stall and looked at the price of the trees. 'Wotcha, kids!' The man who owned the stall came up to us, stamping his feet and blowing on his fingers. 'What tree do you fancy, then?' 'Have you got one about eight shillings?' I asked.

'Now that's not what I asked you, was it? I said, "What one do you fancy?"'

I was confused. 'This one,' the boys said in unison. Of course it was the biggest one there.

'There you go, then, young 'uns,' he said.

'How much is that?' I was dreading the answer.

'Listen, sweetheart, your mother was a beautiful gal, a real lady. It's the least I can do for her little 'uns. Too good to live in this bloody world, she were; a real lady, too. 'Ere, take a "tanga", each an' all, an' one for the baby.'

'Thank you ever so much. Mummy always said how nice you were, she liked you a lot,' I lied.

'Well, God bless you, kids,' he said, wiping a tear from his cheek and a dewdrop from his nose simultaneously. 'Don't tell *him*, mind – bleeding foreigner, I wouldn't give him the drippings from me nose!'

'Thank you, thank you ever so much – and Merry Christmas!' I said.

'Merry Christmas and thanks,' added the boys, without my prompting.

'Not a word to him, remember. Too bloody good for him, she were. I've heard things about him – bleedin' Mick!' the man emphasized.

The boys were struggling with the tree now, as if to get it round the corner as soon as possible, before he changed his mind, realizing perhaps that he'd be giving the 'bleedin' Mick' some pleasure too. We were all heady with excitement, and I said, 'Jimmy, be quick. Go back over to Forrester's and get that snow house!'

We were afraid that someone had snapped it up already, and stood waiting in the biting wind. Soon James appeared with a big cardboard box and a brown bag.

'We'll have to give Dad some change. What have you got in there?' I pointed to the bag.

'Old Forrester gave us two packets of balloons and some chocolate Father Christmases to hang on the tree.'

Patrick and James dragged the tree through to the back yard and leant it against the dustbins, and we were giggling nervously as we walked through the back door. There were no lights on, but when I switched the scullery light on, the fire was burning brightly. The table was laid with sandwiches and cakes, and the cups and saucers had been put out too.

Perhaps Dad was in the bedroom. I took Anna out of her push-chair and put it behind the scullery door.

'Go to the lavatory, Jimmy,' I said. He sauntered out of the door. I was placing our purchases behind Mummy's rocking-chair when I heard James flush the toilet and then come back in.

'He's in the front room!' said James, looking to me for some sort of explanation. I had none to give.

The elation left me. Then suddenly the door opened and he was standing there.

'Well, did yers get all yer wanted?' he was smiling. 'Didn't yers get a tree?'

'It's out by the dustbins, Dad,' said James.

Dad opened the back door. 'Holy Mother, will yer look at the size of der tree! It's bigger than all of yers,' he laughed. 'Take it round to der front door, boys, and we'll bring it in the passage.' He went and opened the front door. I heard him panting as he made his way back in with the tree – he had sent the boys in to start their tea.

Soon Dad came and joined us, and after we had washed up he said, 'Now I want yers all to close yer eyes fer Daddy and follow me.' We walked behind him in a chain. 'Right, yers can open up now,' he told us.

We were in the front room, and although I had too many memories of it to be as happy as the others, as I looked at the fire glowing brightly in the hearth, the standard lamp throwing out a soft light, and the TV still standing on the sideboard, my fear of the room evaporated. It was going to be a good Christmas after all.

The boys were all around their father. He had leaned the tree against the wall, and already the pine fragrance had filled the room. I ran to him and kissed him, and he held me close. 'Please, God,' I prayed, 'let him always be like this.'

'There now, chilluns,' he said, 'go and get yers shopping and we'll see what we'll be doin' wid them.'

He took the box of drawing pins we'd bought, and put up the two pull-out decorations. Then we spent the rest of the night in a human chain, licking and sticking the paper rings together, and passing the chains to Dad, who put them up, looping them all 'just so'. It looked wonderful. Next we had to fill an old galvanized bucket with some of the soil from a bomb-site across the road, adding some bricks to hold the tree steady as Mummy and Gran used to do.

Then Dad said we'd done enough for the night, and we sat drinking our cocoa and writing our notes to Father Christmas. We watched the letters float upwards, all five of them drifting up the chimney with the flames.

14

The next two days were to be as heady as that one. Harvey delivered three hundredweight of coal, and we trimmed the tree and bought crêpe paper to cover the bucket. Joan had called on Christmas Eve with some parcels for us, and we put them under the tree. We were so busy that day that we didn't notice the pile of presents under the tree getting higher.

Dad had given us fifteen shillings each, to spend on presents for each other. I spent most of my fifteen shillings on him, getting a Blue Gillette razor and blades set in a case, and twenty Players from all of us, while the boys bought Players Weights for Ruby and for Gran. We also bought Gran a little bottle of 'April Violets'; James took these up to her, with a card, but she wasn't in, so he left them with a neighbour. The spirit of Christmas abounded now. The boys bought little things for each other, and a tiny dolly that fitted into a matchbox bed for Anna, and these were all placed under the tree. As for me, the boys bought me 'something I'd always wanted', and Timmy drove me mad asking me to guess what it was.

I made several journeys to the shops for sweets and nuts, apples, oranges, tangerines and vegetables, and Dad had gone out and bought a large piece of beef. There were Christmas puddings too, and Ruby bought a load of mince pies.

'Did you make them yourself, Auntie Ruby?' asked James.

' 'Course I did, luv, and these an' all!' She produced a pile of sausage rolls, and eventually a Christmas cake, complete with holly, a snowman and a robin.

'I hate to say this,' whispered James, 'but for Ruby those are all the wrong colour!'

But so what if they were in boxes marked 'Bates the Bakers'. It was Christmas, and Ruby could be excused her fibs!

Dad and Ruby came back later with a bottle of port, lots of bottles of beer, lemonade, Tizer, ginger beer and other things too numerous to recall.

As all children are, we were ready for bed at eight o'clock on Christmas Eve. Ruby had gone home, and we all lined up to kiss Dad 'Goodnight, God bless.' (I'd had to guide him through the rituals of how Mummy 'did' Christmas.) He

97

was going out, but he said he'd try to be back in time to help me fill the stockings that we'd each hung on the mantelpiece.

'Daddy'll be goin' out fer a wee drink later on, chilluns,' he said. 'But mind yer all asleep when I gets back in case he comes down the chimney early and catches yers!' We all laughed.

About half an hour later we were all talking in whispers when he put his head around the door and said, 'Pop up an' do the fire fer Daddy in an hour or so, there's a darlin' girl.'

'Yes, Daddy. Have a nice time,' I said.

'If yer Mammy were here, I might,' he said, quietly. We heard the door shut.

The boys were very excited. First James got up to go to the toilet, then the other two.

'Come back to bed, boys,' I called.

'We're only looking at the tree.'

'He'll kill you if he finds you up.'

'We forgot to put the candles on the tree,' said James. 'We won't be very long.'

'Don't you dare light 'em,' I warned. Anna was just falling asleep. 'I'll kill you if you wake her,' I hissed at them.

'We're just checking we put the milk and mince pies out for the reindeers,' whispered Timmy.

'You know we did. Come back to bed, Timmy,' I said.

Patrick was next to appear. 'Heh, the reindeers'll have bloody lockjaw if Ruby really made those mince pies!'

'Come back to bed at once, you little sods.' They knew I was angry now.

'OK, we're just putting up some more balloons and we'll be in.'

I heard them creep in, still whispering, and I decided I'd better be getting up soon to check those fires. The boys' whispering gradually ceased, and when Patrick, the last, got no response from any of us, he must have drifted off. I wondered what the time was. I didn't really want to go into that room on my own, but I knew I'd have to. There'd be trouble if I let the fire go out . . .

I was dreaming of falling — but my arm had been caught in a mangle on the way down. 'No . . . no . . . no . . .' I'd wake in a minute. But suddenly the dream let me fall hard against cold linoleum and an iron bedframe. Water was dripping over me — no . . . no . . . no . . . Now I was being dragged through a cold passage-way.

'Yer feckin' little bitch, yer feckin' murderin' little bitch, all of this fer yers, all of this, an' this is the thanks I get.'

I was wide awake now. It was a nightmare's nightmare, the front of my head was sore where I'd been dragged through the hallway to the front room. My face was being slapped, side to side, side to side.

'Yer feckin' murderin' little bitch, I'll show yers what sort a' Christmas a feckin' murderer has!' He kicked the tree until it overturned crazily, then he went round ripping down all the paper chains and decorations. He was going to kill me and I didn't know why.

He picked me up from the floor. 'Yer feckin' banshee,' he screamed.

His fist came at me as I went to turn my head, and he caught me squarely on the nose. His hands were covered with blood. Horrifically, strands of blood were looping from my face onto his hands like a dark, dreadful umbilical cord. I tried to get up, and slipped on something wet on the floor. Urine cascaded down my legs.

'Yer've feckin' pissed yerself,' he screamed. 'Holy Mother, why did I have to have a banshee like her? Tell me, Mother?'

He kicked my buttocks several times and I lay there, cold, bruised and bloodied. Then he'd gone. I heard him go into the lavatory and then the kitchen, where I could hear him put the kettle on. He must have had a wash, and after that I heard the clink of a bottle against a glass as he made his way into the front bedroom. Then, swearing, he locked the door.

Lying there, I recalled one of my mother's Christmas rhymes: ' 'Twas the night before Christmas and all through the house, not a creature was stirring, not even a mouse.' I didn't cry, I just lay there, thinking about last Christmas – a hundred years ago, it seemed.

Some time passed. I could hear his snores coming loudly from the next room. At last I got up. Every part of my body seemed to be aching, my face was stiff, and I could only walk with a stiffened gait. I threw some coal on the fire in that front room with my bloodied hands, and then I made my way down to the kitchen, where our empty stockings hung on the mantelpiece.

I pulled the big fire-guard back and put coal on to that fire too, with my bare hands. My mouth was beginning to feel as if I were pouting disproportionately, and my eyes wouldn't seem to open without giving a pinkish hue to everything.

I went into the scullery and put the kettle and a saucepan of water on. My feet were making slight ripping sounds as they trod the linoleum; they were sticky with blood. Going to the cupboard, I took out the 'nosebleed sheet', which had been greatly depleted over the last few weeks. Once again I tore off strips, and filling the bowl with warm water, made my way to the front room.

I began to wash the blood-stains from the wall and skirtings, then from the floor; I wrestled with a stain on the carpet, and then took the bowl back into the kitchen. All this time my nose had been bleeding into the bowl, but now it was stopping, and I emptied the bowl and poured in more water. Once again I went over the blood-stains on the carpets and various splashes I'd missed in the front room. Then, crawling down the passage-way, I washed away the bloodied footprints, tracing the line my footsteps had made until I was in the scullery once more.

Again I changed the reddened water, and stood in the bowl, stripping off the yellow pyjamas Auntie Pam had given me. They had become stiff with blood, as was my vest. I stood there, gingerly washing my face and neck, and all the way down my body. Then, wrapping an already damp towel round me, I walked quietly to the bedroom and put on the white petticoat Auntie Pam had given me, and a navy blue cardigan, the kilt, fawn socks and plimsolls.

As I passed the front room my heart fell as I saw the destruction of the paper chains, now sprawled across the furniture, or just resting on the floor. Other decorations had been torn down, and sat in sad little circles about the room. The Christmas tree looked worst, and some of its glass balls were just gleaming splinters on the floor. After much ado, I managed to scoop up the soil and steady it again with the bricks. The damage to the tree wasn't as bad as I had thought at first; some of the candles had snapped, but only three of the glass balls had broken. I had to sit the new fairy doll on a branch, and she swayed drunkenly to one side.

I collected up the small pieces of paper chain and threw them onto the fire, then I removed the glass and soil with the dustpan and brush. The fire was burning brightly now. I went into the kitchen and began to fill the empty stockings with the contents of the box that was on the top of the cupboard; into each stocking I put an apple, an orange, a tangerine, nuts, a Mars bar and sixpence, and fastened them all to the mantelpiece.

As I reached under the table, my nose started to bleed again and I held the sheeting up to it. I dragged the bags out from under the table, and folding the Christmas serviettes with our names on, put them in order of age: Caroline, James, Patrick, Timothy and Anna. On top of these I placed the three white-netted Christmas stockings meant for the boys, and filled with games, whistles and cars, and put Anna's and my stockings (with cut-out dolls, tiny dolls' mirrors and plastic rings) beside our names. Next there were four lots of blow bubbles for the younger ones, and puzzles of varying sizes for different ages — Anna's was a six-piece puzzle.

My nose had stopped bleeding at last, although my eyes wouldn't seem to open more than half way, and everything still had a pinkish hue. Reaching for some more bags, I found them in disarray — those bloody nosey boys had been at them! The boys had boxes of soldiers, paints and painting books, three bows and arrows with plastic plungers on them, and a game of ping-pong between the three of them. I lifted up the cardboard box and eventually managed to prise out their fort, making room for it at the back of the table.

Now came Anna's bag. She had a soft skin doll with blonde hair and a pink dress, a tiny folding dolls' push-chair which I put the doll into, a pink dolls' tea set and a miniature sweet shop with weighing scales. Sod it! I thought, as I fished around under the table for my own bag and my nose began to bleed again. Eventually I crawled right under the table, but there was nothing with my name on, nothing at all. The only present lying on the space marked out for 'Caroline' was the white-netted stocking. I moved all the toys along, then went outside and looked into every dustbin. Well, he hadn't thrown them away, the bastard!

Something furry wound round my legs, accompanied by a low growl. I jumped. It was Prowler, with a rat in his mouth. I kicked him away, and off he went, with his prey. Then I went into the kitchen and started to peel the potatoes, prepare the sprouts and cabbage, and scrape the carrots. I took the wrapping off the Christmas pudding, put it in a white bowl and stood it in some water in a saucepan. Next I cut some slivers from the beef, putting them on top of the sprout and potato peelings, after which I put the meat in the oven with the dripping on it, ready for roasting. I made up the Yorkshire pudding and covered the bowl.

God only knew whether Dad would get up at all tomorrow. The smell of the Christmas pudding reminded me of Mummy, and removing the beef from the oven, I put it on one side and then put some of 'Ruby's' mince pies in the cooker to warm. This was more like it, I thought, as the smell of the mincemeat and pastry wafted through the kitchen. I went to the cabinet and took out another sachet of Nescafé. Although Dad had bought a tin, I didn't want that; this was mine and no one else's, not even James knew about it.

Prowler was mewing at the window, and I let him in; I'd guessed that he would lose his prey and be back soon. I let him in at the back door, fed him the bits of beef, and put down a saucer of milk.

My head and body were hurting desperately now, and I tore two Aspros off the strip, not even caring if this was an overdose. I downed them through lips that would hardly open, then put some Demerara sugar and some milk in the coffee and tried to sip it. My back hurt badly, but I couldn't see where the injury was, or what part hurt the most; my hips and thighs were already a purplish blue, weals had been raised down my legs, and there were cuts on both legs where he'd dragged me over some broken linoleum. My wrists were starting to go purple where his hands had dragged me, but I was used to wearing my cuffs down.

I must have fallen asleep, for I woke with a start. Prowler had jumped on my lap, and was licking my face; he seemed to sense the hurt, and didn't leave my side for the next two days! I reached for the coffee; it was still warm, but my arm had gone numb, and when I went to move it, the pain underneath it and in my shoulder made me cry out. The room had grown cold. I made the fire up, and took the mince pies from the oven, then I picked up the plate that held the mince pie for the reindeer, and as I couldn't eat, I scattered it in the yard for the sparrows or rats. Taking the milk that Prowler had lapped at, I put it into my father's cup, and made another trip to the dustbins – but there were still just bits of rubbish inside.

The kitchen door was opening. It was James. 'Cor blimey!' he said, as he saw the fort and looked at the mantelpiece to see if his stocking had been filled. Then he turned his eyes on me. 'Jesus Christ, what's he done to you?' he demanded.

'Sssh, Jimmy,' I said.

'What's the fucking bastard done that for? You'll have to go to hospital.'

'No, Jimmy, please no, no,' I begged. 'I don't know what I've done, honestly.

He's knocked down the Christmas tree, ripped down the decorations, and I'm not even sure if we're allowed back in the front room again now.'

James was ashen. He clenched and unclenched his fists. 'Right,' he said, pushing his shoulders back and going into the scullery. The knife I'd just used to cut off some beef for Prowler was in his hand. 'I'm gonna run him through with this.'

'Oh God no, Jimmy. No more, please, I can't stand any more, and we'd both be charged with murder.'

'It'd be worth it,' he said, putting the knife down. 'Look at your face, will you?'

I looked in the square mirror that hung over the fireplace. It revealed a terrible mess. My eyes were purple and closed, my lips were swollen, with congealed blood forming a line around them, and little masses of congealed blood were dotted all over my face.

James was punching the fist he'd made of one hand into the cup of the other. Suddenly he turned to me, his face crumpled; all traces of the little man had gone, and he cried. 'Oh Mum!' he was calling, over and over, 'I want Mummy back.'

'So do I, Jimmy, so do I,' I said, and we stood hugging and comforting each other until at last I said I'd make him some coffee. I opened my father's new tin and made James a cup, heaping it with milk and sugar just as he liked it. He went into the scullery and splashed his face with cold water. Suddenly he was the 'tough guy' again. Then he took from the Christmas tree some of the cotton wool we'd bought, and bathed my face in warm water.

Afterwards we went and surveyed the damage in the front room. James stood and whistled.

'Jimmy, don't say anything if he comes in, will you?'

He didn't answer, but I knew he was as afraid of our father as I was. James rearranged the tree and the tinsel, then, taking a chair, he stood on it and put the fairy back on top. We managed to make a fairly good job of refixing the paper chains (or, at least, James did), and finding a silver ball under the sideboard, James put some new candles in the candle holders. Suddenly his face lit up, and after searching in the sideboard drawer, he came back holding two gold and two silver bells.

'Where'd you get those from, Jimmy?' I asked.

'I nicked them that day we went to Woolworths,' he said.

'Jimmy!' We both laughed as he hung the bells on the branches. He stacked the presents under the tree and found one that had rolled into the corner of the bed-settee; it was obviously a ball for Anna.

'Sorry about the water balloon,' said James, as he stood on a chair to take two broken balloons down.

'What water balloon?'

'Didn't it work then? We set it up for you when you came in the door to make the fire up ... Oh Christ! Did you come in and make it ...?'

'No, Jimmy, I fell asleep.'

'Oh my God, he must've walked right into it. Oh Christ, oh please don't tell him it was me! I'm sorry, Sis, what can I do? I'll do anything to make it up to you, but don't tell him who it was.'

'I won't, Jimmy, but you'd better warn the other two.'

Once again he kissed me, once again he was crying.

Patrick and Tim were standing in the doorway, now. 'He's been! He's been!' they cried.

'Sssh,' said James. 'Get in the kitchen you two, quick.'

They were looking at me, and both mouths were forming an 'O'. Clearly, they were very frightened – it was Christmas morning and my three brothers were scared stiff.

Once in the kitchen, their eyes took in their presents, and then looked back at me.

'Look what he's done to her,' said James. 'She didn't get the water balloon, he must have.'

'Sorry, Caroline.' They were both frightened by my appearance, but they still couldn't understand how I could look so horrific.

'He thought *she'd* done it, so he beat her up,' said James. 'She's not going to tell on us, though, are you?'

'They can't charge people for the same crime twice, can they?' I lisped through my swollen mouth.

Anna was pattering down the hall now. 'Ooh, ooh, dook!' she kept saying, pointing to her dolly and pram up on the table. I put her slippers on and she happily pushed her way through, knocking everyone's shins.

They were all very subdued, and as they took their stockings from the mantelpiece, Timmy cried out, 'Caroline! I want Mummy to come back.'

'So do I,' Patrick joined in. James came over, blinking hard, and put his arm around the boys with me. Anna started crying because the others were, and then, seeing my face, pointed, saying, 'Dook, dook.' She spent the next two minutes alternating between laughing and crying at my face.

'We hate him.' Patrick spoke up for the other two.

15

The lads ate their cornflakes in the scullery, and I fed Anna while she was trying to dip her doll's teacup into her cereal. I warned the boys to make sure they didn't have his cup.

'Why?' They all looked at me.

'Well, it's just that Prowler caught a rat in the night, and then he came in, and I gave him a tasty little snack of beef and a saucerful of cows' milk. What he left is in there.' I pointed down into Dad's cup.

'Oh boy, perhaps he'll get the plague,' said James.

'Or typhoid,' offered Patrick.

'Or the measles!' said Tim. We all laughed.

'Let's all get dressed before he gets up,' I suggested. The boys went in and put on their best jumpers, socks and grey trousers. I dressed Anna in white long socks, a white frilly petticoat, a white lace dress and white cardigan, then sent her scampering back to the kitchen to play with her dolly. I tried to put on my only dress – green tartan with a white lace collar. But my arm was so painful that I couldn't raise it high enough. I abandoned the idea of a dress, and put on an old blouse, buttoned up the navy cardigan again and slipped the kilt back on. No one would notice, I thought, and they didn't.

James turned the wireless on and got Bing Crosby singing 'White Christmas'.

'Merry Christmas, chilluns.' My father came through the door and stopped dead as he saw my face. 'Holy Mother of God! Will yer look at yer poor sister's face? Now whichever of you boys did that silly trick last night? Sure she could well be spendin' her Christmas in the hospital. Now we've all got to take special care of her. Look at her poor, poor eyes, straight on her face she fell as she slipped down on der water.'

'Liar! liar!' I thought. 'How long have you been awake to think that one up? Jimmy is right, it will have to be the crushed tablets, but not in his tea. So in what?' Or was I going mad? An air of guilt and shame hung over everyone.

James poured him a cup of tea, and he sipped it. 'Tis a great cup of tea yer've made yer Daddy too, sweetheart,' he said, sitting me gently in the chair. The boys began to giggle. 'Now then, yer'll see me work some more magic.' Once again the beef was cut into two strips and placed over my eyes. 'Head back, darlin', there's my girl.'

Anna started to cry. It was a confusing morning for her, but she joined in as Dad and the boys started to laugh at me. Soon he made us all ginger-beers and put some sugar in Anna's as I'd shown him, to take out the fizz. Then he went back through the front room and returned carrying the coal scuttle. He made up the kitchen and front-room fires too, and next he took the scuttle back, and with the carpet sweeper in one hand, made his usual speedy clean through the front room in five minutes flat. After he'd polished, we were all ushered into this room while he made a start on the kitchen.

The boys brought their fort in and the soldiers, but Anna kept bumping it with her tiny push-chair. 'No, m'darlin', you're coming with Daddy,' he said to me. Our bed had been made and a hot-water bottle was between the sheets. He brought two Aspros.

'I took two in the night,' I said.

'Sure, it won't be hurtin' yer.' He went out, and came back with a cup of tea and a straw. ' 'Tis a funny thing yer Auntie Ruby should have brought these for der younger ones', he said, indicating the straw.

'Mmm,' was all I could say, as I sipped the tea through the straw and felt sleep overtake me at last. One by one the others sneaked in, and in a very dazed state I asked sleepily, 'Look at my back, Jimmy, please.'

'Oh my God! You've been kicked all over, it's black in some places.'

'Thas' OK, Jimmy, I thought I was going mad.'

It was Jimmy who later came to wake me. 'Come on, it's dinner time, and I think we've got one of the reindeers staying. I can't say whether it's Donner or Blitzen!'

'What you talking about, Jimmy?' I managed to lisp.

'Just come and see,' he said, taking my hand to help me out of the bed. I was so stiff now, and in so much pain, that uncharacteristically James began to look worried as I moaned.

'I think I need Dr Scanlon,' I said.

'Oh Christ,' he said, looking both worried and scared. I crept slowly along the passage, wincing with every step.

As I came into the kitchen, it was to a heroine's welcome, as if I were a veteran returning from the war – which I suppose I was in a way, 'Here she is,' they were saying. Anna came and sat on my lap, but she was ill at ease with me.

The house smelled of Christmas now; the pudding was steaming, and the aroma mingled with that of the roasting meat, and the pine tree. The table was set with the familiar silver, and Mummy's serviette ring was amongst the rest that encircled the white linen. Crackers were strewn across the table, and a wine glass was placed at each end, with a bottle of red wine standing next to each. Four cups were placed alongside the other four settings, two on each side of the table, while Anna's high chair held a plastic beaker, her silver pusher and spoon, and a cracker.

Suddenly Ruby emerged from the kitchen, carrying some plates heaped with food. It was then that James's wisecrack about the 'reindeer' hit me, and I felt the blood ooze from my mouth as an involuntary chuckle escaped from my painful lips. Ruby was indeed 'Ruby' that day – she wore a red velvet dress with a full skirt; there was white fur round the cuffs and neck, and although her black 'skull cap' had disappeared, leaving all her hair the same brassy colour, it had been parted in the middle and two girlie hair-slides with red butterflies standing up like antlers!

'Ooh, my gawd, yer did go a wallop, luv.' She looked very concerned. 'I'd get Scanlon t'ave a look at 'er, Terry. – Merry Christmas anyway, darlin'.' She rested her chin on top of my head and kissed the air. 'C'mon you lot, it's on the table,' she called.

I tried to lift Anna into her high chair, but James came to the rescue. He'd found a piece of tinsel and put it round her head like a halo, and she was obviously delighted with the result. God knows how I sat through that dinner. I couldn't eat, and though my father even cut up my food as he had done for Anna, it wouldn't go down. He'd filled up his and Ruby's wine glasses several times, and as the meal continued he became even more generous and poured some into the boys' cups. Soon their cheeks were flushed. Anna was a diversion for me as I helped her eat her dinner; even she had been given wine, though with some sugar and topped with lemonade.

Dad and Ruby insisted that they clear away the first course, and as Dad came back in, carrying the pudding which was giving off blue flames, even I became fascinated. 'Cor!' the boys exclaimed, time and again.

'How did you do it, Dad?' asked Patrick. Another Christmas-card illusion had become a reality, though minus the sprig of holly or the robin – and the flames weren't exactly red and orange. Dad brought half a bottle of brandy through from the kitchen as the other flames died away, and pouring some of it over the pudding, he set light to it and the flames turned orange briefly, before turning blue and dying. 'That was great!' said the boys as Ruby bustled in with a jug of custard.

As the pudding was cut, the piece with the lucky sixpence enmeshed in its dark, treacly mass came to me. Everyone clapped. There were no sulks this year, and they all seemed genuinely pleased that I got the 'lucky' sixpence.

My father was pressing me to drink some wine as I hadn't touched the main course and had only taken small amounts of custard and miniscule pieces of pudding. I raised the cup to my lips, but the wine tasted foul and it caused my lips to feel as much aflame as the pudding had been. 'Get her a straw, Tel,' said Ruby, who'd become one mass of flame. Her cheeks were so flushed that they seemed to be on fire, threatening to burn the yellow thatch of hair.

I accepted the straw, though it didn't make the vinegary taste any better; but by the time I'd drunk another half cup, I was starting to feel warm inside and the pain was beginning to dull. Once again we were told to leave Daddy and Ruby to wash up, and go into the front room. Logs were crackling on the fire in there now, and remembering the snow-house, I pulled it out of the sideboard and placed it on top of the mantelpiece.

A Jack Benny show was on the TV, and as Dad and Ruby came into the room, giggling like two schoolgirls, she suddenly started singing in a tuneless voice, 'Can it be the trees that gives the breeze this rare and magic perfume ...' Jack Benny didn't stand a chance.

Anna was sleepy and James took her into the bedroom. I lisped that I wanted to lie down. I felt light-headed, and the room started to spin sickeningly as I put my head on the pillow. When I awoke, it was dark and I was alone. I lay there for a while, the tears falling down my cheeks as I remembered, then both Patrick and James came into the room, switching the light on, which alarmed me almost as much as the torch. I could only see mistily now.

'You OK?' James asked. I nodded.

'Tea's ready,' said Patrick softly.

'Where is it?'

'In the front room as usual,' said James.

'Boys,' I managed to whisper, 'I didn't get any presents.' I began to cry helplessly.

'What do you mean?' said James in his masterful 'I'm gonna do something about this' voice.

'Not one,' I sobbed, discounting the net stocking.

'We got you one,' said Patrick, and as he began to cry, he ran from the room and we heard him lock the toilet door.

'Don't say anything, Jimmy, please,' I begged.

'No, I'm going to ask.'

'Wait for me, Jim,' I said. He helped me out of bed again. I dried my eyes on the rough kilt, which made them even more sore, and, holding his hand, followed James into the front room. The sideboard was laid out just as Mummy and Gran used to set it. There were beef and salmon sandwiches, mince pies, a Yule log – and Ruby's Christmas cake in the centre. The TV had been put on the floor, and Mummy's trolley was set with cups, saucers and side plates.

'Here's Daddy's poor baby,' said my father. He got up from where he'd been sitting on the sofa next to Ruby. Anna was trying to pour water from a doll's cup into her new dolly's mouth and didn't even look up. 'C'mon, sit down next t'yer Auntie Ruby, darlin'.'

He was about to call the boys in for the Christmas tea when James said, surprising and frightening me at the same time, 'My sister hasn't had any presents.'

'Sure she has, m'boy,' Dad said, patting James on the head. 'Sure, she's not looked hard enough. – C'mon now, you chilluns,' he called. I could feel the tears stinging my eyes again, and I made an excuse to go to the toilet. I could hear someone outside getting their coal in as I sat on the toilet seat. My arm and my shoulder felt as if they were weighted.

I rolled back my sleeve and looked at the markings round my wrists and forearm; they had taken on the shape of chipolata sausages, but the colours were purple, blue and green. Not for the first time I wondered if it was worth carrying on and not admitting to the police what I'd done. But then they'd take me away from Anna and the boys, and I couldn't bear that.

Someone was knocking on the toilet door. 'Yer all right in there, dearie? I'm dying for a pee, an' there's gonna be a bloody flood aht 'ere unless you 'urry!' I flushed the toilet and came out; she smiled at me with her broken teeth and danced her way past me, saying 'It'll be all dahn me leg, *an'* a bootful in a minute!'

I went back inside, to find my father swaying dangerously near Anna as he tried to pour the tea. 'Pick her up, Patrick,' was all I could whisper to my middle brother. He immediately picked her up, and I pointed to the settee, where he put her down, though she complained bitterly. The tea was distributed, then Ruby made a big ritual out of cutting the cake, insisting that she and 'Tel' (which seemed to be the name my father had newly acquired for Christmas) cut it together.

This time it was the boys who were sent packing to do the washing up, and they did so without a murmur. Meanwhile I sat uncomfortably on the settee with Dad and Ruby, while Anna, who'd had very little contact with me that day, pushed her pram around the room, babbling at her dolly all the time. When the boys came back in, it was time to open the presents under the tree, and as he began to hand out the gifts, calling the boys' names and Anna's, he suddenly reached behind the settee and dragged out the box that had held the boys' fort.

'Well, will yer be lookin' at this, chilluns?' We all stopped. Here's yer sister's presents.'

With great deliberation he handed me a pair of pink slippers with bobbles on them, a crushed brush and comb set, a pink nightie, a tin of 'Muget' talc, and a pack of playing cards. All of them were covered in coal dust.

'An' will yer look now, they've got soot on them. He must've been in a fair hurry comin' down the chimney.'

'Thank you,' I said, putting my cheek, which he kissed several times, near his face.

'No presents, indeed, an' yers been such a boon to yers Daddy, eh?'

Patrick, Timmy and Anna took a closer look at the soot. Timmy shrugged, but Patrick sat down again beneath the tree and finished unwrapping his presents. Ruby had bought the boys cap guns, which delighted them until they discovered there were no caps. Anna had a celluloid doll with a cloth body, and Ruby bought me a necklace of red glass beads. Joan had brought me a *Girl* annual, the boys had the *Eagle, Dandy* and *Beano* annuals, and Anna had a pop-up Cinderella book. Then from Auntie Ruth I had a manicure set, the boys had a clockwork train set between them, and Anna had a panda, while Granny's presents were a game of draughts between us, the ball for Anna, and a knitted scarf in blue for each of us, in our varying sizes.

(I wondered how Granny's and Auntie Ruth's presents had got there; one of them must have called, but we hadn't seen them. An overwhelming desire to see Granny again brought back the tears which I had begun to dread.)

'Now look an' see what yer Daddy's got from Auntie Ruby,' said Dad, holding a navy blue jumper in one hand and brandishing a bottle of 'Navy Rum' in the other. I noticed he'd only made a tear in the holly-patterned square package that Granny had sent for him, just big enough to establish that it was forty Senior Service.

'An' now it's Auntie Rube's turn to show off,' she said. She produced a gold powder compact with blue flowers over it. 'Ain't it posh, kids?'

We all pretended to appreciate that it was indeed 'posh'. Our father was madly beckoning to James, who I saw take a flat wrapped parcel with a Father Christmas on it; Dad motioned to him to give it to Ruby.

'Well, Ruby, this is from the chilluns.'

'Oh, 'ow lovely,' said Ruby, tearing at the paper. We were all as curious as she was to discover what 'we' had bought her. There was a half-pound box of Black Magic chocolates and a pair of nylons. 'Oh, yer little luvs,' she said.

James sprang forward, handing our father his razor set and cigarettes, and Ruby her Weights and some bath salts (which I'd thought it was wise to buy, as the cigarettes hadn't looked much on their own). For the next five minutes we were kissed and called 'little darlins', 'angels', 'Tel's credits' (by Ruby), and 'Daddy's darlins who had hearts of gold'! James was sent off to get two glasses and some cups, and while we had Tizer, Dad and Ruby were filling their glasses with rum.

'Now what da yers do?' Dad asked.

'Turn the lights out and light the candles on the tree, and sing carols,' James said.

'That sounds just right,' said Dad.

We began to sing – or at least they did – and after a rendering of 'Hark the Herald Angels Sing' which Ruby managed to mutilate as she'd done the previous songs, he began to sing 'Silent Night'. The others joined him at first, and suddenly stopped; he was singing solo, and so lovely was his voice that we were all captivated as he finished 'slee...eep in heavenly peace', his voice reaching the beautiful high notes without wavering.

We all applauded him, and he finished with the 'Londonderry Air', which held us equally captivated. Ruby was crying and blowing her nose. There was a lump in my throat, and tears were wet on my cheeks; in the strange light I could see that his were wet too. 'For I'll be here in sunshine or in shadow . . .', he'd sung, and that was what he was – 'sunshine and shadow'; a voice that was so beautiful it could fill you with sunshine, and yet so menacing that it could send you into the shadow of great terror.

The tree lights were blown out, and it was decided that the snow-house would be opened on Boxing Day.

'Hey Tel, make the kids one o' them coffee cups from Ireland,' said Ruby.

'Irish coffee d'yer mean, darlin'?'

'Yeah, tha's right, Tel.'

'Tel' went out into the kitchen and brought back a tray with four cups and a beaker for Anna. 'Yummy!' the boys all said, and drank it straight down. Anna took about three sips and fell asleep on the floor, but not before she'd given us some dances as the boys put the tinsel halo on her head, and Dad and Ruby sang 'Dance, little dolly, with a hole in yer stockin'.

'Eh, Tel, there's gonna be a 'ot time in the ole town ternight, eh?'

James took Anna into bed, and one by one we said our goodnights. In the sanctuary of the bedroom James and Patrick whispered, 'Where did your presents come from?'

'Well, they didn't get messed up down the fucking chimney!' said James.

'He'd put them in the coal bunker,' I lisped. 'It was coal dust all over them.' I told them how I'd heard someone outside when I'd gone into the toilet.

'I wish we could've had a chicken, and if I'd got the wishbone he'd be dead now,' said Patrick.

'We'll have to work out that plan, Sis,' whispered James.

'What plan?' asked Patrick.

'We'll tell you tomorrow,' promised James, but we never did.

Anna woke me the following morning, and if anything I seemed to be stiffer and the pain in my shoulder worse. Anna was wet. She pattered beside me down to the kitchen, where, to my surprise, the fire was blazing and Ruby was just coming out of the scullery with a cup of tea in her hand, and a cigarette hanging from her mouth which seemed a totally different shape without the scarlet paint.

' 'Ang on, kids, I'll get yer a cuppa, and she turned back into the scullery.

I poured Anna's 'cuppa' into her bottle and took her wet nappy off.

'Sit dahn,' Ruby insisted. 'I'll git 'er − what is it − them rusks?'

'Yes please,' I lisped.

The boys appeared presently, and Ruby sat them all down and gave them cornflakes and tea. It was while I was dressing Anna that James had the temerity to ask, 'You been here all night, Auntie Ruby?'

'Good Gawd, no! I went 'ome straight after yer wen' ta bed.'

I'd listened to them singing 'White Cliffs of Dover', 'I'll Be Seeing You', 'Don't Fence Me In' and many others, amid Ruby's guffaws well into the early hours.

'Never off duty, yer Auntie Rube,' she said, brushing down the now badly wrinkled 'ruby' dress.

Boxing Day passed with a lunch of braised beef and a tea similar to that of Christmas night, and the only treat was that we could watch the television. However, there was a final high spot − the opening of the snow-house. There were six tickets inside, three blue for boys' presents and three pink for girls. Dad insisted that Ruby should have the third pink ticket which, to her delight, was a light-goldy-coloured metal ring which was chipped a bit around the gold and had a big emerald 'stone' in the middle. Anna's hair-slide and my plastic bracelet went unnoticed as Ruby jumped around the room, showing her present off as if it were part of the crown jewels.

'D'yer know, kids, this 'as bin the 'appiest Christmas of my life. I lost my little gel in the Blitz, an' me 'ubby didn't come back from the War neither, an' yer've made me so 'appy.'

We all said good night to them, leaving them to drink a bottle of whisky this time. Out in the kitchen James was mimicking Ruby. 'Me 'ubby didn't come back from the War neither, cos he 'ad 'is bleeding 'ead screwed on – not arf!' It still hurt me to laugh, but laugh I did, fit to bust.

The rest of Christmas found me 'confined to barracks'. Not once did I go out, and even when Gina called (to show off her presents, no doubt), my father told Patrick to say I was in bed with a cold. On New Year's Eve he came back with Ruby, drunk. They saw the new year in by getting us out of bed and opening the front door to let the old year out and the back to let the new year in. This resulted in four sleepy kids freezing in a circle with their hands crossed, grasping other hands, and singing the words to 'Auld Lang Syne'. We were each given some beer, and went hazily back to bed. The worst year of my life had ended. Or was it to be the worst?

16

By the end of the first week in January, my injuries had healed considerably, leaving now only yellow-brown bruises that were fading fast. My shoulder still hurt but the pain was only there now if I lifted Anna up on the wrong arm. My first trip out was to the library and to get some meat from the butcher's for a stew that Ruby was making.

It was on the following day, when I went into the chemist's to change Dad's prescription from Dr Scanlon, that the kindly old man asked to see how the finger was doing. I still had a livid scar, but it had nearly closed; the old man seemed pleased, but once again decided to pull it together with Elastoplast.

'What happened to your eye?'

'Oh, the boys were making water balloons and I slipped ...'

I was surprised that there were any bruises left on my face, but perhaps our forty-watt bulbs had given a different picture in the mirror to that shown by the daylight. I quickly pulled my sleeve down as he finished dressing my finger, but not before I'd seen him look at the yellowed wrist.

'Thank you very much, and a very happy New Year,' I said. I ran from the shop and nearly forgot to buy the vegetables in my rush to get home.

We had been back to school a whole week when I started a nosebleed in the middle of a geography lesson. I was quite pleased, because I hated geography, and when it didn't stop after five minutes, and some blood had fallen on a textbook, Mrs Marsden, the teacher, sent me to the school nurse. Two hours later it still hadn't stopped – or at least, as soon as we thought it had stopped, it would start again.

'I think I'm going to have to send you home, my love,' said the nurse, 'and then straight on to the doctor. Is there anyone at home right now?'

'Yes, my father will be there,' I assured her.

'You've lost quite a lot of blood, and I think it will be best if I pop you home in the car. I'll just go and let the Head know.'

This was the third time I'd got into a private car, and the nurse told me it was an Austin 7 when I asked 'What is it?' I hadn't quite meant it that way, but as she had not taken offence, I added, 'It's little and lovely too.'

'Now I'll just come in and explain to your father that we need you to see a doctor,' she said, as we arrived.

'No, no, Nurse, really – thank you ever so much, but Dr Scanlon's coming to see Daddy this afternoon anyway. I think that's his car – yes, it is,' I lied, hoping she wasn't familiar with a vehicle that I wasn't even sure existed. I'd never seen Dr Scanlon drive a car.

'Well, don't run, my love. Let me know what the doctor says, won't you?'

'Yes, Nurse, and thank you ever so much.' She stood watching me walk through the dark entrance to the Mansions, then I waited until I heard the car drive away. I ran round the back way through the yard and was met by Prowler. He'd had no Kit-E-Kat for days, and I was feeling guilty. 'I'll take some bottles back and get you some food this afternoon, boy,' I told him.

As I walked through the scullery into the kitchen, I noticed the fire was dying down. The wireless was on, and I wondered where my father was. I went to the cupboard and tore a strip from the 'nosebleed sheet'. There was only a little bit left now, but I held that up to my nose and put the thick gauze pads the nurse had given me on a sheet of newspaper, ready for when he took me to see Dr Scanlon.

I went up the hall to our room. The beds weren't made, and the front room door was open, though there was no one in there. I stopped outside Dad's bedroom door and thought I could hear him snoring softly. I opened the door. For a second or two my eyes didn't seem able to grasp what it was they were looking at — blond, brassy hair with black roots, fat white thighs spilling over suspenders, and black stocking tops embedded in flesh, one large long breast hanging, crowned by an enormous brown nipple, and his buttocks white and muscular, exposed.

'Oh Christ, Tel! Get orf, get orf!'

I turned and ran, the 'nosebleed sheet' in my hand, the blood running, feeling almost hot now, as it came down my nostrils.

'Come back yer feckin' little bastard, I'll be tellin' ...' It was all I heard as I ran blindly into the passage way that led to the exit from the Mansions.

I walked the back streets to Granny's slowly. She wasn't home. I spent some time in the comparative warmth of an underground station, where I went to the Ladies and washed off the blood which had dried on my face (the bleeding had stopped now). I was about to throw away the sodden piece of 'nosebleed sheet' when I thought better of it and put the rag in my pocket.

There was a sixpenny piece in my pocket, and I went into a run-down café and bought a cup of tea for tuppence. I sat there for as long as I could, and only left when the man in the dirty apron asked if I wanted anything else — like a bed for the night! I was pleased to see it was time to collect Anna from the nursery — well, it was only half an hour early; I collected her, but had to carry her as we'd gone there by bus that morning and there was not enough money left to catch one home.

All the time I was thinking of what I'd seen in that bedroom and it seemed in my muddled mind almost as bad as the afternoon when Mummy had died. It was somehow just as frightening, but in a way I couldn't define.

'Mungry, Mummy Caroo,' Anna was saying, so I went in and bought two bars of Cadbury's chocolate with the last fourpence.

We walked as far as the big department store that I'd been to with Granny and Joan, and I tried to remember what bus Granny and I took from there to go to Auntie Ruth's. I knew she lived in Hampstead. It was dark and Anna was crying, and as I walked up the long hills and turned off according to the directions that various people gave me, I was becoming desperate. I knew there was no going back now, so I turned to make the long journey to Joan and Dennis's office. I'd just have to take my punishment. How long would they send me away for, I wondered, as I fed bits of the chocolate to Anna. Would the boys and Anna be allowed to see me?

Suddenly a car pulled up alongside the kerb, and before I knew what was happening, a policeman was coming towards me.

'Caroline? Come on, love, don't be frightened, we're not going to hang you.' (Oh God, he'd told them!) 'Get in the car, darling, your little sister's going to catch her death.' For the second time that day I got into a car.

'You've got everyone worried sick, you have. Here you are,' said the policeman who was in the driving seat, throwing a blanket over into the back of the car. I wrapped Anna up and held her close to me.

'Do you want to tell us what happened, darling? Come on we've heard you're a tough little thing, must've been something nasty to make you run away.'

'What's he going to do to me?'

'Who?'

'My Dad.'

'Has he done anything to you already then, love?'

'No.'

'Are you sure?

'Yes.'

'We won't tell him anything you tell us, you know.' Silence. 'Well, if you change your mind . . . I've got a little girl your age, she's a bit like you. Except she's got a mum too, she talks to her mum a lot.' Silence again.

'I tell you what, we'll come in with you now, and if you change your mind and want to talk to me or Len here, you just come into the station — or, here, I'll give you the number, you can ring us up and me or Len here will come and pick you up, and I'll take you to my house for tea, to meet my girl and my missus.' He was writing the number down. 'Just ask for PC Doug Smith or PC Len Johns, and if we're not there, or if we're off duty, we'll tell them at the station to ring us at home. All right, darling?'

'Yes, thank you very much,' I said. Anna was asleep. As the car stopped, the policeman who'd done all the talking gave me a bit of paper and told me to hide it in my pocket.

Anna didn't wake as the policeman with the little girl took her from my arms. She had been a dead weight, and my shoulder was hurting again, as if 'he' were in some way reminding me that he would be here with me always.

'Whad'yer reckon, Len?' I heard the policeman carrying Anna whisper to the driver of the police car.

'I reckon it's pure Billingsgate,' the other one said, as he took my hand and then knocked loudly on the door. I was terrified and wished the policeman would stay and hold my hand forever.

It was Joan who answered the door and put her arm around me. 'Thank God you're safe, my love. Come into the warm.'

'Is there a cot to put this precious bundle in?' asked the policeman carrying Anna.

'Probably best to bring her through to the kitchen where it's warm,' said Joan.

Dad was sitting at the kitchen table. He'd obviously been crying, and the boys were hunched around the fire looking terrified. He jumped up when he saw me and took me in his arms.

'Oh darlin', darlin', don't ever do this to yer Daddy again, I thought I'd be losin' my mind.' He was kissing the side of my face when he moaned in my ear very softly, 'not a word'. He released me, and Anna, who had woken, started to cry.

'Put the kettle on for warm drinks for yers sisters — and the officers, of course. Or would yer be wantin' somethin' a bit stronger?'

'No thank you, sir,' said the policeman with the little girl. 'We'd just like a word with Miss Bowden, if we can go somewhere for a few minutes?'

'Sure yers can.' He ushered them all into the front room, then came back and made a great fuss over Anna and myself. The boys were looking bewildered. James and Patrick knew it must have been something pretty terrible to make me leave them, and as Dad went into the scullery to make us all some tomato soup, James whispered reproachfully, 'Why didn't you take us?'

Dad came in and placed the soup in front of us with a plate of bread and a plate of biscuits. He was pouring tea, and I was feeding Anna when the policemen came back with Joan.

'Well, we'll be off now, sir. Eh, you lads are looking down in the dumps! Tell you what, the next time we've got a few minutes and we're not busy, we'll take you boys out for a ride in the police car. Good idea, Len?'

'We'll see you all, then, and don't think you girls are the only ones who get taken home in style in a police car – can't leave these fellas out.'

'Can we ring the bell?' asked Tim.

'It'll have to be somewhere away from people, like, but I don't see why we can't arrange three little rings. And don't forget what I told you, young lady,' he said, pointing a finger at me and winking.

'Bye, sweetheart,' they were waving to Anna. She waved her spoon back at them and spattered Patrick with tomato soup.

'Gee, thanks!' said Patrick.

Joan was drinking a cup of tea. 'Bye,' she said to the policemen.

'They were nice coppers,' said James.

'Yeah,' agreed the two other boys.

'I can't be thankin' yers enough, officers ...' He was putting on his usual routine as he escorted them to the door. As he came back in, Joan asked if she could have a word with me in the front room.

'What happened, Caroline? Please tell me.'

'Nothing happened,' I said.

'Caroline, if there's something going on or happening that's made you act so irresponsibly towards not only yourself, but also that young sister of yours, whom you kept out in the cold and dark for all those hours, you must tell me. There are your brothers too, who have been so upset, and your father. The police have been looking for you for nearly two hours. Your Grandma is frantic. And you expect me to believe nothing happened! So if the mood takes you again, you'll repeat this performance, will you?'

'All right,' I shouted, 'I'll bloody tell you, you never come here, and you always promise, and then you've got too much on at work!' I could feel the words rising in my throat, but at the same time caution took over. 'I had a nosebleed today. It bled for two hours and the school nurse brought me home so that Dad could take me to the doctor. There was no one here, so I ran away to see if Granny would take me, but she wasn't home either – she never is – so I collected the baby and tried to find Auntie Ruth's house!'

'OK, sweetheart, OK, I'll take you to see Dr Scanlon myself tomorrow. I can see you don't believe me, but I'll be here at 8.45 to take you and Anna to the nursery, and then we'll go and see Dr Scanlon. And look, if you think I was being harsh, just now, it wasn't because I wanted to hurt you any more than you've been hurt already, or frightened by the policemen. What I do want you to do is to have a little think. If things are too much for you, then you can tell me anything at all that may be worrying you. It doesn't have to be now, tomorrow will do, or in a few days – and it doesn't need to go any further than you and me.'

This was the second offer that evening by someone who wanted to help me share my troubles. Or was it that they knew, all of them, because he'd told them? Could it be a conspiracy between Joan, the police and Dad to get a confession out of me? Well, I wouldn't be phoning PC Smith (or the quiet one) at Canonbury Police Station, and Joan could have her answer now. I wouldn't be giving any of my secrets away – and most certainly not *the* secret. I was already being punished enough by my father.

My father had now become a figure that represented, not violence, but something that was maybe even more frightening, though it was hard to define. I knew I would never ever feel the loving things that I used to feel for him, even after he hurt me badly and then asked for my forgiveness. It had all changed, but I didn't know why.

'Come on, sweetheart,' said Joan, 'I'll stay till you're in bed tonight.' I suddenly felt frightened to think of her staying here alone with him after we'd gone to bed. I didn't know why, and I certainly couldn't warn her – but those were the words that came to mind – 'warn her'!

The next morning Joan came and collected us in the black Hillman car, and after taking Anna to the nursery, we went along to see Dr Scanlon. A week later I went to see an ENT specialist, and two days later I had my nose cauterized. Nothing more was said about my 'escapade', and Ruby was never seen again.

17

From that time on, my father went round the house cleaning it; day in, day out, the windows would be polished. I still took the washing to the bag-wash and got the coal from Harvey's coal yard. When someone stole the push-chair from outside the laundry one day, while I was waiting to collect the wash, life became a bit more difficult. Dad would leave me to drag the big white bag home unaided; my arms never quite reached round the bundle so that I could carry it, and even when I did try to carry it, I couldn't see where I was going. Though the coal was more compact, it was just as heavy, and equally difficult because my shoulder still felt bruised.

I had a week off school after I had my nose cauterized, and during that time, apart from his frenetic cleaning, Dad seemed just indifferent – not only to me, but to the boys and Anna too. I would limp back from Dr Scanlon's after he'd given me my iron injection (he'd found I was anaemic), and my father would just take the paper, cigarettes and shopping from me, and make me a cup of tea, with a vague smile.

I was beginning to think that his tantrums were easier to live with than this, and yet I could feel a strange undercurrent. One morning, as I went to get the coal in, I found that the coal bunker was half filled with bars of broken white wood, and it wasn't until I saw the wheels on the end of a thicker piece that I realized it was Anna's cot.

There were never any extra pennies put down on the table for 'sweeties' these days, but the boys collected newspapers and sold them at an old yard. They'd made a cart out of some old pram wheels and a plank of wood, and they steered it with a piece of my old skipping rope, though they only made about sixpence even when it was loaded to look as if it carried the produce of half of Fleet Street. That cart also came in handy, while the novelty lasted, for taking and collecting the bag-wash and coal, and the boys were occasionally paid for doing the same for the occupants of a neighbouring street. They thought business would thrive, but it didn't, and once again they had to rely on the returns on Tizer and lemonade bottles.

One Saturday a letter came, addressed to me, in blue type. 'I knew it, I knew it!' I thought excitedly. I'd sent in a poem to the *Girl* comic and the prizes were postal orders for 10*s*. first, 5*s*. second, and 3*s*. 6*d*. third. I waited until the boys went out to play, savouring every moment until I could open it – I could imagine my name in print at the end of the verse already! Leaving Anna to give breakfast to her dolly, I sat on Mummy's rocking-chair, and opened the letter carefully. As I pulled out the sheet of paper, I noticed it didn't have the *Girl* logo of a girl's head in profile, blond hair trailing behind her as if she were running.

And then, once again, I couldn't absorb what my eyes were telling me. It was in the same blue type, just the one word: *MURDERER* it said. I screamed, startling Anna, and threw the letter on to the fire; then thrusting the envelope after it, I watched as the flames dissolved the last corner of the stamp bearing the Queen's head. I wished it was my head burning now, in hell-fire, as one day it surely must. As I stood there watching, I found I could no longer cry; the one scream had been enough.

Joan started to collect Anna from school about once a week, and on that day I would be dispatched to one doctor or another. The front room was no longer out of bounds, but none of us ever went in there any more, as Dad spent most of his evenings alone in there, talking to 'the other side'. At first it had been very scary; we would hear his voice raised, saying, 'But, Irene, don't be so stubborn about this, can't you see I'm trying to protect them, darlin',' or 'Well, make up your mind, Irene darlin', d'yer want "China Doll" or "These Foolish Things"?'

The thing that I found most chilling was when he started laughing, and I'd wonder if Ruby had returned. Sometimes it sounded as if she were really with him, and he'd say, 'Darlin', yer always had two left feet.' Each night now, as we lay in bed, he'd end his 'conversations' by singing 'Good night Irene'. Out of nervousness, we would whisper in the dark that he was hoisting Ruby out of the window; we even used to say 'This is Terence O'Farrell signing off now ...' and then sing 'Good night Irene'.

Another letter came for me, with the same blue printing, and I wondered this time if it was from Scotland Yard. Were they trying to wear me down? I'd seen films about the War where people had been brainwashed. This time I didn't open the letter, but threw it straight on to the fire, checking and double-checking that it was gone as I crushed the ash over and over with the shovel.

One evening as I came back from Muswell Hill (it was one of the evenings when Joan was collecting Anna), I noticed that what I had been given was not a prescription but a letter addressed to my father. He smiled as I came in and handed him the letter, but when he opened it, his face quickly changed, making my heart jump. Then he threw the letter on to the fire as I had done with mine. After we'd had tea, when I was putting the washing around the fire-guard to dry, James came in and said Dad wanted to see me.

I went into the bedroom and noticed that he was trembling and holding his chest. I felt the familiar throb in my spine as I approached him. He put out his hand and held mine, still clutching his chest with the other hand.

'Daddy's got some bad news from the doctor in the letter yer brought me. He says yer Daddy's gettin' worse.' His breathing became more laboured, as if to emphasize the point. 'It's yer cat, darlin', that's makin' Daddy suffer more, an' this doctor – he's a good man, sure he is – he tells me der cat must be put down.'

I stood trembling. 'Prowler?' I asked, incredulously. 'But he wouldn't do anything to harm you!'

'Sure he wouldn't, an' Daddy knows how much yers love him, but yer see, t'the good doctor my life is more important than an animal's. Now don't be cryin' so, or yer'll have Daddy cryin' too.'

'But I won't let him in ever again,' I promised, 'I'll never let anyone hurt you Daddy, I'll do anything, anything in the world, but please, please let me keep him, I love him so much.' I was on my knees now, I was begging.

'But darlin', darlin', it isn't just a matter of keepin' him locked out, even if we could. However hard Daddy cleans – yer can't see it, and no more can I, but bits of fur are all over the house, an' it'll take time as it is, but eventually it will all go away and Daddy will be able to breathe better. A long, long time ago it was that Hammersmith Hospital told me he must go, and now 'tis best to get it over wid. Yers can hire a basket from der pet shop in der morning, an' yer'll have the bus fare there an' back an' Daddy will be waitin' for yers. He's goin' to join Mummy, yer know, sure he is.'

'But I didn't tell about Ruby ...'

'What'd yer say darlin'? Ruby's gone for a holiday to her sister, sure she'll be back soon. Is there somethin' about Ruby tha's been troublin' yer? Is it tha yer'll be missin' her then?'

I nodded my head. Maybe this would mean a reprieve.

'Well, don't yer be upsettin' der boys wid such bad news. I think it'll be better if we kept this as another one of our little secrets, darlin'.' He kissed the top of my head, and I stood up. In silence my soul screamed, 'God, Holy Mother, I'll go to Purgatory, I know that, but please not Prowler!'

Dad got up and told me to get some cigarettes for him, and some Tizer and crisps. I ran into Forrester's, and ran out again as he began to ask what was wrong. 'Don't let anyone be kind to me, God,' I begged.

I walked along the alley-way that ran along the back of our yard, beyond which lay the backs of the shops. It had an odd smell of fish, meat that had been cooked, bread that wasn't quite bread, and the pleasant smell from the chemist. Among the litter of old tins, bottles, boxes, mud-encrusted paper and excreta, there lay the occasional dead rat, and sometimes a decomposing cat that had been run over could be found. Everything littered this alley.

'Prowler,' I called, 'Prowler.' Two large creatures scuttled past my feet in the dark, but I couldn't find the cat, and I was in danger of being heard by my father if he was in the kitchen. I ran back, doubling around to our back yard and went in at the back door. He was telling the others some stories of the 'old country' and was more animated than he had been in a long time. He asked me to go out once again and get a piece of cod and chips, which I did, and this time I searched along the front of the shops for the cat. When I got back, Dad offered the chips round and ate a little of the fish himself, wrapping the other half up in the newspaper.

The boys wanted to know why I'd been crying again and the only thing I could think of to say was that the School Board man had been to see Dad.

'That's not your bloody fault,' said James. 'He keeps you off, the old bastard. Anyway, why wouldn't that quack give him any pills?'

'What do you mean, Jimmy?' I asked.

'Well, it's bloody obvious he's not going to throw a prescription into the fire, isn't it?'

I hadn't thought about that too much, and I began crying softly in the dark. Then I heard Prowler outside, and the back door being opened, followed by Dad talking softly to the cat. I woke early the next morning, to find Prowler sleeping next to me. He was stinking of fish.

'Go away, Prowls,' I said, giving him a gentle shove off the bed. It was then that I remembered. I wondered if my father had got any pills; perhaps if I got him some, and reminded him that Mummy had brought Prowler for me, he would change his mind.

When I arrived in the kitchen, I found two half-crowns on the table, with a note which read, *I've gone to see Dr Scanlon. Please do as I asked yesterday, as the doctor is going to check up that this has been done. Love from Daddy.*

The basket with Prowler in was heavy as I carried it towards City Road where the PDSA was. I'd been there before, when the cat had been badly cut in a fight and Mummy and I had taken him in, probably in the same basket; we'd brought him home with a little less fur and some big black stitches along his side. He was making much the same frantic scratchings then as now, when we took him on to the bus, though then he'd been bleeding so badly that Mummy had had to fold a whole sheet for him to sit on.

Suddenly I made a swift about-turn and began walking first in this direction, then in that, through Georgian houses with their little square communal gardens, and council flats and terraces. On and on I walked, until I came to a row of three shops; there was a butcher's, a post office and a grocer's. I released the big staple on one side of the basket, and before I could begin to open the other, Prowler was gone in a mad panic. He flew one way as I flew the other. It took me about an hour to find my way back to the main road, and then I got on to the first bus that came along, not realizing it had stopped for the traffic lights.

'Hey, darling, I should put you off for light jumping,' the conductor said. 'Ain't your Mum told you it's dangerous? – What you got in there, then, eh? I bet it's a monkey. Give us a look.'

'No, it's empty. I had to have my cat put to sleep.' I was trying very hard not to cry again.

'Old was he, darling?' said the clippy sitting next to me and the basket (which took up two seats).

'No,' I sobbed.

'Eh, it's not the end of the world. You'll get another one, ask your Mum. I expect he had the mange or something.'

I held out my fare. 'Nah! Save it for a new cat,' he said, 'and hope to Gawd the inspector don't get on.'

I got off at the next stop, though I had quite a bit further to walk, and took the basket back to the shop; they gave me back the deposit of 3s. 6d., minus 1s. charge. Then I took the money back to my father and gave him the receipt from the pet shop.

'I'm sorry, darlin',' he said, 'but it had to be done, for Daddy's sake.'

Now there was another job for me to do in the mornings, he said. He was very sorry, but I'd have to go to the doctor and collect Dad's tablets for the day, before I took Anna to the nursery. Each day I would have to collect the tablets, except for the weekends when he'd get them doubled.

That night I told the boys the real reason for my tears the night before, and told them that I'd done a turn-about in the City Road and had finally left Prowler outside a butcher's.

'He should be strung up, that bastard,' said James; it had become his catchphrase.

'Who?' Prowler?' asked Tim.

'Go to sleep, Timmy,' said James. 'What about the plan?' he added cryptically.

'Why don't you tell us about this plan?' Patrick complained.

'Because we haven't planned it yet, dummy,' said James. 'I was wondering about Marmite. He eats that on toast, and that's bitter.'

'Not much chance of that,' I said, and I told James about having to go down to Scanlon's for the tablets each day now.

'That's funny. Makes me wonder if he's as bloody ill as he says he is. What do you mean *every* day?'

'Yes,' I told him. 'Except on Saturday when he gets a double helping!'

It was two days later, when I was feeding Anna, and the boys were getting ready for school, that there was a scratching at the window – so familiar a sound that no one noticed. It was only as I went to ask Tim to 'let him in' that the full impact of what had happened hit me. The boys were overjoyed to see him, and Anna tried to catch his tail. We gave him some milk, and James started to sing, 'But the cat came back, the cat came back, we thought he was a goner, but the cat . . .'

'Did he now, by all that's feckin' holy!' Dad was grabbing my hair, and Anna screamed. The boys huddled closer together. 'Yers didn't have a thing to feckin' do wid it, like lettin' the bastard free?'

'No, no, please, he must have run away from the PDSA, he must have done.'

'Yers'll tell the feckin' truth or it's all up wid yer. Would yer like me t'tell 'em all what they've got here? Sure, they'll want to be lynchin' yers themselves if they're sons of mine. Tell the truth, did yers free this feckin' animal?'

'Yes. Yes, I did.'

'Yer filthy, lyin', murderin' bitch!'

'Yes. I don't care any more if you do tell, he's mine and I love him, and I did let him go.'

His grip tightened even more cruelly on my hair, and now with one resounding slap across my face, he let me go. The boys were all crying, and Anna screamed as she saw me crash into the table from the force of the blow.

Then suddenly he altered again. Somehow he managed to bathe the boys' eyes, and he put his arms around me.

'Forgive Daddy, please forgive me boys, I've not got me pills. Now rinse yer eyes, James, and you two.' The boys immediately obeyed. 'Now, James,' he went on, 'will yer be goin' round to get a crusty loaf, ten Players and the Mirror – and there'll be change enough for a tanner each, sure there will. An' James, be sure an' get yer Dad his tablets from Scanlon. Take Patrick wid yers, and Tim, 'tis best yers go to Scanlon's, James, and take this note to him.'

The boys trotted off, looking guilty at leaving me behind. I usually ran the errands, except for sweets, and they were apprehensive.

'C'mon t'yer Daddy, darlin'.' He was bending to pick Anna up from where she was hiding beneath the rocking-chair, but she screamed as he approached her. 'Yer murderin' feckin' banshee, yer've turned my own baby from me, sure yers have!'

He was trembling again and I thought, as his hand stretched across to me, that he was going to hit out at me again. So did Anna, because she gave a loud-pitched scream and buried her tiny head in my tunic skirt.

'It's just a sixpence I'll be givin' yers. When yer come back from the school – not yer school, mind, yer'll not be attendin' again today, an' I'll just have to tell the School Board when he comes here again, yer were off playin' truant again. No, when yers have taken the baby to nursery, yer to come back here at once, d'yer hear? Now, that sixpence is for a tin of cat food for yer animal's last supper.' Then, putting another three pennies on the table, he said, 'This is for yer feckin' fare up to da nursery. If I'd me own way, it'd be bare footed yer would be walkin' there an' back!'

The boys came back as I was leaving. 'Get a tin of Kit-E-Kat for Prowler,' I said to James.

'Christ, we'll be late,' he said.

'At least you're going in. He's been telling the School Board I've been playing truant!'

'Bastard!' said James.

'Is Prowler staying now?' Patrick asked.

'I honestly don't know,' I said, dishonestly.

James came back with the blue Kit-E-Kat tin and, panting, pushed the boys through the door. 'We're late. Move!' he ordered them.

I followed them out, and Anna was late for nursery too that morning. As I walked back I thought, 'If I murdered Mummy, he's going to make me murder Prowler too'. Why had he said 'the last supper'? I was soon to find out. Prowler was sitting on the hearth rug, having a good wash after his meal as I got in, and the other purchases the boys had made were on the table.

'That's more like it, Scanlon, yer ole bastard,' Dad was saying; he had obviously got extra pills. He turned to me. 'Now, yer murderin' little bitch, yer used to this, so I'll be makin' it swift for yers. I've heard it said that when yers have killed once, 'tis easier the second time. So here's a note to the PDSA, explaining why it's to be done, an' requestin' a certificate that the cat has been put to sleep — just like yer put yers Mammy to sleep.'

He handed me a ten shilling note and told me to get to the pet shop for a basket on the double. It was a bigger basket this time, and heavier. I put it in the scullery, but Prowler seemed to sense he was in danger. He made a dive towards the living-room door and eventually got under the cooker. Dad crawled after him. 'Yer little bastard,' he said, as he eventually caught hold of the screeching animal. His hands were badly scored — and so was my heart, with Prowler's screeches.

My father sat on the basket, doing up the straps at each side, and when it was secure, he remained sitting on the basket and lit a cigarette, getting his breath back. Prowler's pitiful cries could still be heard and his frantic scratching grew louder.

The pain in my chest seemed more crushing with every step I took on that last journey. I went up the steps at the dispensary, and sat among people with a variety of pets in their arms; some creatures were in shopping bags, and there were another two in big baskets like the one I was holding. A lady with a spaniel was trying to make conversation. Now and again I heard her say things like 'He's my life, he is . . . this canker is a bleeding nuisance . . . '

It was my turn. I went into a smelly room, and a young man took Prowler from me. Not once had he let up in his scratching and his fight to escape.

'Can you find a home for him?' I asked the young man. I'd given him the letter, I knew I must, but he seemed kind, and I wondered if I could do a deal with him.

'Well, dear, this letter — from your mother, is it?'

'No, my father. My mother's dead.'

'Well, the cat seems to be a health hazard and I've been asked to put him to sleep. Asthma, is it?'

'No, only cancer,' I replied. 'Please don't let him die, I love him so much.' Prrowl, prrowl was coming from the inside of the box, and the tearing of wicker could be heard. 'Please, please let him live, he loves me too . . . he sleeps with me . . . he licks my face when I'm hurt . . . I love him so much.'

The young man was looking flushed. 'Look dear, I know this is heart-breaking, but he won't know anything, just a little prick in his fur' . . . (just a little knock on her head) . . . 'and he'll be in a wonderful sleep.' He was easing the basket out of my hands.

'Can I see him just one more time, to say goodbye', (before you put him in a room with yellow curtains, his mouth sagging open at one side).

'No, my dear, it's better not, he'll know you're here and with him.'

'Prowler . . . I love you!' I could still hear him mewing and scratching as the young man pressed a button. A lady appeared.

'Take the little girl upstairs for a cup of tea, Jean,' he said.

'Come on love.' She took my hand.

'I love him, I love him,' I kept on repeating. She gave me a cup of tea.

Half an hour later, having paid one and ninepence, I was given a note, which I read while sitting on the basket. The note said: *One male cat (tabby), 7 years old approx., destroyed by injection of* . . . (I couldn't read or pronounce the drug that had killed him) *at 11.35 a.m. on 7th February, 1957. Signed . . . Veterinary Surgeon.*

18

That night, in bed, we all cried bitterly, but I told a fib to save the others some of the pain.

'He's going to try and get him a new home,' I lied.

'But what if he comes back again?' asked Patrick.

'Oh, not in this country,' I lied. I cried for most of that night. There were cramping pains in my stomach which I thought Dad had caused when he pulled me backwards by my hair. As I carried Anna into bed that night, the pain was cramping again, and I felt my bladder go involuntarily. I ran into the bathroom as quickly as I could, my pants were getting wetter all the time. I hadn't even felt I wanted to go – perhaps it was the kick at Christmas or just the shock of losing Prowler.

I went into the toilet and took down my navy-blue school knickers; as I did so, I saw, (with shock, excitement and fear all rolled into one) that it was blood running down my legs, soaking my knickers. I wanted to tell someone, but there wasn't anyone to tell, so I wiped away the dampness at the insides of my thighs, where the blood seemed to be pouring. All I could use to wipe it was my knickers, which I placed between my legs.

I felt more of the warm flow seeping from me as I went into the kitchen cupboard. There was no 'nosebleed sheet' left, so I took one of Anna's cot sheets, hacking at the flannelette material with a knife. With difficulty I tore two strips off, then, taking a folded piece, I placed it between my legs. Then I heard Dad's footsteps coming towards the kitchen and scullery, and dropped the heavily stained knickers behind the scullery door.

He came in just as they'd fallen from my grasp and said, 'What did yer just put down there?'

'Nothing – er, the floor cloth.'

'Well, pick the feckin' floor cloth up, an' put it under the sink, c'mon, c'mon.'

'I can't.'

'Well, I don't think for one minute that yer'd think about lyin' to me again, but yer've taken to disobeyin' me now, have yers?' He hit me hard across the face, and I reeled towards the scullery window, while he bent and picked up the navy-blue knickers. 'Ah, so 'tis a floor cloth, is it?' he said.

The piece of cot sheet had fallen from between my legs, and a large oval patch had spread over it.

'Oh! So yers have started yer monthly flow, have yers? Answer me, yer little animal. Am I to take it that yer stinkin' bloody drawers are to be found there in the future, just for any one of us to pick up for yer feckin' ladyship? Yer a dirty, filthy, little bitch on heat, 'tis all yer are. D'yer know what happens to young animals who leave their mess behind? Well, I'll be feckin' showin' yers now, 'tis the only way t' teach 'em that others aren't goin' to pick up the mess for them.'

I'd sunk against the back door now, cowering, and I could feel the blood drip, drip, drip on the floor. He pulled me up by the hair, then, holding my head back, he smeared the blood all over my face and hair. Then he went away. I took up the cot sheet and put it quickly between my legs, in case he came back again.

There was a tap on the back door as soon as I had locked it. 'Who is it?' I asked, trying to put the other piece of cot sheet under the cold tap, then washing my face and hair, and trying to dry myself on my tunic.

'It's me. What's the back locked for?' It was James. 'Oh Christ, not again,' he said.

'Go into the kitchen, Jimmy, while I clean up,' I told him. He went through.

Next I heard Dad come through and speak to James. I wondered if he was telling James what I'd done and, if so, whether I could ever face my brother again. But I heard them both leave the room. I put the kettle on to boil and tiptoed into the kitchen. There was no one about. Quietly I opened the kitchen door and crept up to the hall. Next I took some clean knickers out of my drawer, as well as the yellow pyjamas that Auntie Pam had given me. They were still marked with a coffee colour from other blood-stains.

I crept back into the kitchen, and poured the warm water through my face and hair, then got to work on the rest of my body. I folded the cot sheeting back between my legs, put my pyjamas on, and then stood in the bowl to remove the blood that was etched between my toes. Then I rinsed the bowl again and again with disinfectant, and did the same with my knickers until the water ran clean. Just as I came back from the yard after hanging the knickers on the line, James came in at the door. I wiped the blood up with the floor cloth and rinsed it as I'd done with the other items.

'What did he hit you for this time?' asked James.

I couldn't tell him, but just said, 'Because I think he likes doing it'.

'Sit down, I'll make you a cuppa,' James said. He took one in for Dad.

'Did he say anything to you?' I asked.

'Like what?' James looked blank.

'Oh, about coming in so late,' I suggested.

'No, he gave me half a dollar for coming in safely.'

'But why?' I opened my mouth to speak, but nothing came out.

'Oh he sent me up to Finsbury Park, to that other quack he's got, and that one gave me a bottle full of pills for him. I got lost though. Some clever bugger misdirected me.' We drank our tea. 'He's happy,' said James. He's playing Mario Lanza – "I'll walk with God" – that's the last bloody person he'll ever walk with.'

We washed our cups and put the things out for the morning.

As I waddled up the hallway to bed that night, the bulk between my legs was very uncomfortable. I hoped James wouldn't notice. In bed, I snuggled up to Anna; Tim, as usual, was over next to the wall. We'd all three of us slept in this single bed for months now, but because of the events of the evening, it suddenly seemed extremely small, and I felt squashed.

In the morning I made the boys their porridge and tea, then fed Anna and got her ready for nursery. I'd had to tear the cot sheet into a much smaller strip and place it between my legs. Later on I'd go to the school nurse, just as the other girls did, but now I buried the soiled piece that I'd used during the night, deep in the dustbin.

Then I took my father his cup of tea, knocking several times on the door. He lay on the bed where once I'd seen that ugly entanglement of limbs, blond hair on black; the memory was still vivid. His arm lay across his eyes, and the empty bottle of pills stood beside a glass with an inch of beer in it. Two or three pills were scattered on the bedside table.

I closed the door, and said, 'He's sound asleep, thank God. Do you want another cuppa anyone?' I threw his cup down the sink. No more would I run to the phone box outside the library. No operator would ask me which emergency service I required. There was no emergency as far as I was concerned.

At school the nurse put a packet of pads in a carrier bag for me, and told me I was a little woman now. When I came out, Joan was waiting in the black Hillman car.

'Hello, Caroline. Get in love, we'll go and pick up Anna. There's a bit of a problem at home, so I'm coming around to sort things out.'

When we got there, Joan knocked on the front door, then knocked again.

'I'll go round the back,' I said.

'No need. Someone's coming.'

'Oh God!' As the door opened, I stood there in disbelief – it was Granny. I threw my arms around her. It was months since we'd seen her, and she looked as if she'd been sliced in two, so thin was she. There was an aura of sadness about her, even when she was kissing me and the baby (who didn't seem to remember her at all, but didn't complain when Granny took her in and smothered her with wet kisses.)

'I'll get the boys,' I said.

'Are you deaf, Caroline?' smiled Joan. 'They're in the front room, and the boys are playing blow football. Now, Gran has agreed to stay with you all for a few days until we can sort a few things out.'

'Are you going to sleep here, Granny, too?'

'Yes, darling.' Her voice too was frail now.

'Is Dad ill again?' I asked, not looking up.

'I'm afraid so. He's pretty poorly.'

The next two days were heaven. Granny let us eat whatever took our fancy, and whenever we fancied it. Auntie Ruth came down with home-made meat pies and some Danish pastries. She brought us all new shoes and socks. A man in a uniform came to see us too, and asked us a lot of questions. He had someone else with him who didn't wear a uniform, but asked most of us questions. The man saw each of us separately after talking to us all together, and James and Patrick must have said something, because they asked if my arm still hurt.

We all had to go along to a clinic and be examined, and after a doctor (not Dr Scanlon) had looked at me, I was sent for some X-rays. The doctor asked if my shoulder hurt, and I said 'only sometimes now'. Then he took out a ruler and seemed to be measuring the cuts (or at least the scars of the cuts) that had been across my fingers.

People seemed to be coming to see us all of the time, and we were never without sweets, or some treat. On the evening of the second day, Joan and Dennis came with a nice couple called Mr and Mrs Paton. They brought a puppy with them which they left out in the car until the boys begged them to bring him in. Tim was delighted with the dog, and told everyone it was a 'baby Lassie'. Then another two people came, a Mr and Mrs Andrews, with their little boy Stephen, who acted as if he was really spoilt the whole time.

The next day, a Thursday, Joan came, and asked the three boys if they would like to spend the weekend with the Patons. I sulked, while the boys asked if the Patons had a garden or a swing. They had a garden, but a swing could be arranged, said Mr Paton. They lived near a river, and he was going to take them fishing.

'Timmy can't swim,' I snarled.

'Well, that's another thing we'll have to see to before long. There's a swimming bath just down the road.'

'Is it in the country?' asked Patrick.

'Half and half,' Mr Paton replied.

Just after the Patons left, Dennis came in with Mr and Mrs Andrews who invited Anna and me to stay at their house for the weekend. I felt rotten then about how I'd behaved to the Patons.

The Andrews' house was really beautiful. It stood on its own, and there were a great many rooms. The room I remember most was the one that didn't have a television in it, but did have a big dark piano which I knew was a baby grand. There were long, dark-red velvet curtains and a big wooden sewing box that was the same colour and as highly polished as the piano.

The only thing I didn't like much was that, although I had a lovely room, it wasn't as big as Anna's, which had a cot and a nursery bed (I'd never seen one of those before). It also had two chests of drawers edged in gold with a matching wardrobe and a deep-pink carpet. All the cot covers and bed covers were white, with pink satin ribbon running through them. The room was two doors along from where I was supposed to sleep, and it was a long way for me to go and get her when she woke up.

My room was decorated in green, with a dark-green carpet and apple-green bedcovers, and the chest of drawers and wardrobe were light-coloured wood, but one thing I did have that was the same as Anna's was a gold lamp with tassels on the shade. This stood on a little cupboard in the same white and gold that was in Anna's room.

It seemed a better idea and less trouble for them if Anna slept in my room, as the bed there was much bigger than the one I had shared with Anna and Tim at home. The next night they said we would see how we got on in separate rooms, but as I had warned them, she woke up screaming for me, and Mrs Andrews had to come in; Anna wouldn't stay in the white room.

The Andrews' little boy Stephen, who at first just showed off all the time, soon became friendlier when I started telling him about the things the boys did. He'd never even been out 'guying', and I told him how all us kids had had our own pitches by the tenth of October.

When we went back to Granny on Sunday night, she'd only just got back from Auntie Ruth's and had brought all our school uniforms back, washed and pressed. (Our other clothes had been cleaned by the Patons and the Andrews.) Auntie Ruth had sent us some sandwiches and cakes and fruit, and with these we spent the evening sprawled about in the front room, watching the TV. We only had to make a cup of tea and a bottle for Anna.

Granny seemed to have cheered up a lot, and told me that Mrs Andrews was coming to take Anna to nursery the next morning, and collect her that afternoon, to give us all a break. On the next few evenings when Mrs Andrews collected Anna, I even began to walk home at a leisurely pace with some of the girls from school.

On Wednesday Joan was waiting at home. I could sense that something was wrong and I expected her to take my hand and tell me to be a brave girl because Daddy had died. The big suitcase was packed and the other little one that Auntie Pam had given us was being filled to the brim too. All manner of strange bags and things littered the front room.

Joan did eventually take my hand and tell me to be a brave girl, but not because Daddy had died; it was because the boys were all going away to stay with the Patons. The boys were very excited, but all clung to Granny, Anna and myself, crying bitterly before they left. Mr and Mrs Paton had brought two silver bracelets, a tiny one for Anna and a larger one for me. They stood in the hall and kissed us both, telling us, Anna and I, that dreadful tale of 'coming to stay in the summer'. How long were the boys going to be gone for, for

God's sake? That night, with no voices to whisper to each other in the dark, the single bed felt very big. I cuddled up to Anna, and Granny must have heard me crying, because she brought some warm milk with nutmeg, and stroked my head until I fell asleep.

Two days later the Andrews called, and I told Mrs Andrews how empty the flat was without the boys, and how Anna called for them. There was an uneasy silence, and then Stephen suddenly said, 'Mummy, I hope we're taking Anna home soon. Julian's coming round at six o'clock for tea.'

'Well. dear,' said Mrs Andrews, 'we're only taking Anna away for a few days to give you a break, so that you can get sorted out.'

But I hadn't packed anything, I thought. Once again my spine throbbed. I began to put her nappies and little baby vests and all sorts of rubbish into old carrier bags. I reached into the kitchen cupboard for her new jumper and her old siren suit for playing in. What about her bottles? What would she do when she woke up and found I wasn't there? Where was her little lamb? I was sorry, but they would have to call back for her sleeping bags ...

Mr Andrews took her dolly and push-chair out to the car, while I pleaded that it wouldn't really be giving me a break. Perhaps I should come with her for a couple of days, to settle her in. Meanwhile Anna was sitting on the rug in the kitchen, playing with some bricks, and Granny and Joan were standing behind me while I searched for some rubber pants.

'The thing is,' I said, 'you can put her in that cot for an hour, and bang on the hour she'll wake up, and one of the ways to get her back to sleep is to stroke the bridge of her nose.' Did Mrs Andrews know 'Ma Curly Headed Babby', I wondered; that was one of the best songs for getting her back to sleep. But if it was her teeth, I was sure that there were some Steedman's Powders up in the cupboard.

'Mummy Caroo, dook!' called Anna. She had found the new Christmas fairy, and she clasped it to her. I bent down and picked her up, holding her close. Now I saw that she was wearing new shoes, not the ones that Auntie Ruth had brought.

'Come on, let me take her from you. She gets heavy.'

'No, she sits just right here.' I smiled nervously at them all.

Why wasn't Granny saying something? Why was she just lighting cigarette after cigarette, and pulling her apron up to her face as if it was mid July instead of the beginning of March, and the perspiration was too much for her.

'She sometimes likes a Farley's Rusk at night,' I said. 'In milk — cow's, not sterilized. And she can only have zinc powder on because ... '

Mr Andrews had taken a couple of the bags now, and Mrs Andrews and Joan seemed to be signalling to one another. Suddenly Mrs Andrews took Anna from me.

'Caroline.' It was Joan's arm round my shoulder. 'You've got to be a brave girl.'

'I must find those powders,' I said. 'She's a bit sore at the moment.'

'Kiss your sister,' interrupted Mrs Andrews, kissing me herself first.

'Mummy Caroo, dook!' Anna was clasping the fairy. She kissed me and we rubbed noses, which made her chuckle. Then Mrs Andrews was walking swiftly away with her, up the hallway. All the bags I'd packed stood there, her unwanted past in the hall. I looked at Joan. 'She's not coming back, is she?'

It was then that I really understood. 'Anna!' I screamed, racing after them. But the car door was closing, and then the car was moving off and gathering speed. I knew she was crying for me. Anna my baby, the boys, Prowler — I ran after the car and tripped.

Steadying myself against the cold red brick of the Mansions, I watched the car and Anna disappear forever. The Pied Piper had played his sweet tune and my world had followed. My mother, Prowler, the boys and now Anna. They were destined to be my ghosts. Ghosts of yesterday.

Later I lay in bed alongside Granny, on the last night I would ever spend in my home. Mummy ... you were all our tomorrows. But tomorrow would be the first day of the next four years of my life. A life in care.

HONNO — The Welsh Women's Press

Honno has been set up by a group of women who feel that women in Wales have limited access to literature which relates specifically to them. The aim is to publish all kinds of books by women, in both English and Welsh including:

> fiction, poetry, plays, children's books
> research on Welsh women's history and culture
> reprints of out-of-print titles.

Honno is registered as a community co-operative. Any profit will go towards future publications. Shareholders' liability is limited to the amount invested. So far we have raised capital by selling shares at £5 each to approximately 300 women from all over Wales and beyond. We hope that many more women will be able to help us in this way. Buy as many as you can — we need your support. Each shareholder regardless of number of shares held, will have her say in the company and one vote at the AGM. Although shareholding is restricted to women, we welcome gifts and loans of money from anyone. If you would like to buy some shares or if you would like more information, write to: Honno, 'Ailsa Craig', Heol y Cawl, Dinas Powys, De Morgannwg CF6 4AH.

Biographical Note

Born in England in 1945, Carol-Ann remained in 'care' following the conclusion of the book until she was sixteen. Her first marriage at that age resulted in her first three children. Unhappily the marriage failed and for many years Carol-Ann and her children faced homelessness.

In 1972 life took a dramatic change whereby she found herself working for a housing association, and security followed when she met and married her present husband David, an architect. She now has five children and three grandchildren, lives in Penarth, South Glamorgan, and is at present writing the sequel to this book.